Treasures of Darkness

Margaret Jank

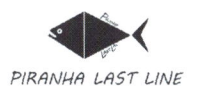

PIRANHA LAST LINE

Originally published by Moody Press under the title:
CULTURE SHOCK

Subsequently published by New Tribes Mission under the title:
MISSION VENEZUELA

Copyright © 2017 by David Jank

All rights reserved. Except in the case of brief excerpts in articles and critical reviews, no part of this publication may be reproduced, distributed, or transmitted in any form or by any means without the prior express written permission of the publisher.

Piranha Last Line is an imprint of Last Line Publishing

Inquiries may be directed to:
info@lastlinepublishing.com
www.lastlinepublishing.com

ISBN 978-1-947777-02-6
(previously ISBN 0-8024-1679-9)

*To the many who prayed for the touch
of God on the big savannah and
were never privileged to
witness the answer.*

Isaiah 45:3
And I will give thee the treasures of darkness, and hidden riches of secret places, that thou mayest know that I, the LORD, which call thee by thy name, am the God of Israel.

Contents

Chapter	Page
Map of area	6
Preface	7
1. Contact	9
2. The Big Savannah	20
3. Marching As to War	53
4. The Battle Begins	70
5. Something New	96
6. Ripples	121
7. The Long Road to Peace	139
8. Tempted and Tried	161
9. A New Sun	179
10. Sweet Sorrow	195

Map of area

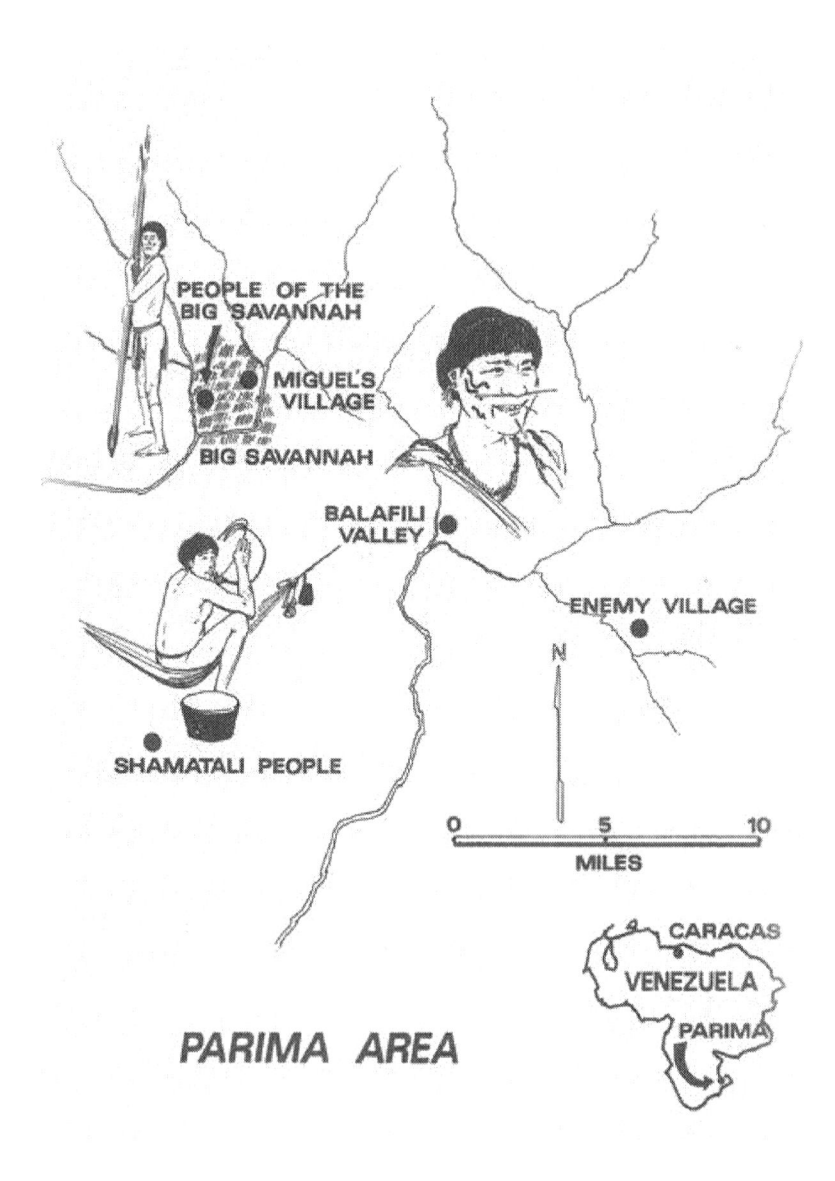

PARIMA AREA

Preface

"Stand still a moment," I once coaxed a Yanoamö friend. "I want to take your picture."

He hesitated and asked me why I wanted it.

"Because you look so nice that way," I replied, admiring his jungle finery. "My people have never seen such beautiful decorations."

He studied me uncertainly. "All right," he agreed, striking a typical pose with his bow and arrows clasped tightly to his chest. "But don't tell them I'm beautiful. Tell them I'm fearless."

Long after the picture was taken, I savored that remark, inwardly applauding the unshakable poise and confidence that typified his entire way of life.

My husband Wally and I first heard of the Yanoamö one wintry night in 1959 when we enrolled at a missionary training institute operated by New Tribes Mission. We listened spellbound as Cecil Neese, returned missionary from Venezuela, shared his adventures among this remote tribe. There were thought to be thousands of Yanoamö scattered over some thirty-thousand square miles of jungle, many of whom still believed they were the only people on the face of the earth.

Our imaginations were completely captivated by a people that could embrace such contradictory extremes of temperament. Their innocence of life's sophisticated evils seemed almost childlike, but they were deadly in their own intrigues. And we marveled, as Cecil spoke, at their indomitable spirit. Not only did they obviously prefer their own way of life, but they seemed to pity the unfortunate few they had encountered who could not claim such a superior heritage.

We tried to keep calm when Cecil told of the need for more missionaries among them; we did not want to look like brash, new enthusiasts. But our hearts were pounding with excitement.

Three years later we met the Yanoamö and spent our first term of service familiarizing ourselves with tribal customs and language in a village that already had been introduced to civilization. Then we joined the Derek Hadley family at a new location in the heart of Yanoamö territory.

Four villages had come together on a spacious, rolling savannah to provide a strong defense against a common enemy in the neighboring valley. For some, the trauma of our arrival had been softened by a contact with the outside world a few years earlier. The rest viewed us with an astonishment that could hardly have been greater had they suddenly been invaded by a family from outer space. The feeling was almost mutual.

The Yanoamö we encountered on the big savannah had practically no exposure to the outside world, and it showed. We quickly concluded that the culture of their lowland kinsmen must have already undergone considerable modification. Never had we seen such an exciting, animated, determined people! Armed with arrows and witchcraft, they were ready to battle the world. They faced the problems of life head-on, and the only enemy to which they bowed in utter despair was death. That, fortunately, was one problem for which we had a solution. We had the message of eternal life.

We became hopelessly entangled in the affairs of our irrepressible neighbors, and they captured our hearts completely. Their response to the gospel was as enthusiastic as all their other responses, and they laid hold on heaven's promises with an exuberance that made us tremble. Their faith was a challenge to our own, and their happiness in the Lord confirmed the fact that the Gospel of Jesus Christ is relevant to the whole wide world.

1

Contact

To preach the gospel in the regions beyond.

2 Corinthians 10:16

The steady whine of an outboard motor broke the stillness of the jungle, and a primitive dugout canoe rounded a bend in the narrow river. Dan Shaylor, a young American missionary in his mid-twenties, sat at the motor and scanned the dense foliage that hung over the water. His friend and co-worker, Paul Dye, searched the bank from the prow for any sign that would indicate they were approaching the village they sought.

Between the two sat five friends who had volunteered to help contact a remote group of Yanoamö tribesmen hidden beyond the reach of civilization. Cecil Neese, the missionary who just several years earlier had challenged us to consider ministry to the Yanoamö, was to accompany them as far as they could travel by river. Then he was going to take the dugout back to the mission station at Tama Tama. The other four were Yanoamö men from lowland villages on the fringe of tribal territory.

The big savannah of the Parima mountains–a wide, natural clearing in the jungle highlands–was to be their final destination. It was an area notorious for its violence, and the sober group in the canoe was well aware of the hazards that might be encountered along the way.

An aerial survey had pinpointed the location of the village they were nearing, and they hoped the noise of their arrival would attract the people to the bank of the river. A series of rapids farther ahead was going to make the river impassable, and it was imperative that they find someone from this village to guide them on their inland trek to the big savannah.

All eyes were suddenly drawn to a large, green palm leaf lying on the bank—a leaf too heavy to have been carried there by the wind. Someone had passed that way. Dan cut the motor back quickly and pointed the nose of the dugout toward the shore.

Pajarito, leader of the four Yanoamö aboard, grabbed his gun and sprang from the prow of the canoe as they brushed against the shoreline. While the others secured the boat to an overhanging tree, he and Paul scrambled up the bank. Seasonal rains had left the ground soft and muddy, and it took only a moment to discover footprints leading away from the river.

"This way! Over here!" Paul called softly, and Pajarito quickly fell into step behind him.

They walked in silence, and while Paul kept his attention on the tracks before them, Pajarito surveyed the surrounding jungle for wild game that might provide their next meal. Suddenly he froze in his tracks and shouted in alarm in the Yanoamö language, "Don't shoot! DON'T SHOOT!"

Paul looked up quickly and came to a halt. Twenty feet before them, a naked, painted savage stood on the trail eyeing them silently down the length of a deadly, six-foot arrow.

"Don't shoot!" Paul echoed with quiet calmness. "We're friends; don't be afraid." Both he and Dan were children of missionary parents and had experienced life among the lowland Yanoamö since their teens. They knew the danger they faced in an area where all intruders were considered enemies, and they were well aware of the fears that drove the Yanoamö to such unpredictable extremes. But their ability to express themselves in the tribal tongue gave them an enormous advantage.

The lone warrior blocking the path before them did not answer for a moment. He studied the gun in Pajarito's hands and said, "Put down that thing you're carrying."

"Go ahead," Paul nodded as Pajarito hesitated. "Take it back to

Contact

the boat."

Pajarito hurried back to the river, and Paul turned again to study the man before him. Bamboo plugs were pushed through his pierced earlobes, and the crown of his head had been shaved in typical Yanoamö style. From head to toe he had been smeared with a bright red dye, and a wad of tobacco leaves bulged beneath his lower lip.

The powerful bow in his hand bent into shooting position, and if he had released the arrow he held in his fingertips, Paul would not have had a chance. But he did not seem to realize his advantage. He was obviously terrified by this sudden encounter with the outside world. Perhaps it was Paul's size that intimidated him. At six foot two, Paul towered a foot above him. The warrior began to tremble violently.

"We're friends," Paul repeated. "Don't shoot. Put down your arrow." The arrow was slowly withdrawn, and by the time Pajarito returned with Dan and the others, their new friend was willing to approach them and inquire as to the purpose of their visit.

Paul told him that they had already traveled four days from Tama Tama, their mission station on the Upper Orinoco River, and explained their two-fold objective. They wanted to reach the big savannah, and they wanted to vaccinate as many as possible along the way against an epidemic of measles that had already devastated many of the lowland villages. Their host was much more impressed with the immunization program than with their proposed trip to the highlands, but he agreed to help them locate the rest of his hunting party to see if anyone would be willing to take them inland.

The following morning they left the area with two reluctant guides, who promised to take them as far as the Shamatali village a day and a half's walk south of the big savannah. But that was as far as they would go. From there on, other helpers would have to be found. The people on the big savannah were dangerous, and the guides had no intention of getting any closer than that.

Three days later they reached Shamatali territory. The long trek into the highlands had taken its toll, and slippery mountain trails had thoroughly exhausted them. They had long since had to abandon their dugout because of extensive rapids, and Cecil Neese had returned with it to Tama Tama, where other missionaries were anxiously awaiting news of Dan and Paul's progress.

They stopped outside the Shamatali village and dropped their heavy packs to the ground while their two guides prepared themselves for the colorful entrance that always highlighted the arrival of visitors in a Yanoamö community. The guides rubbed their bodies with an oily, red dye, and carefully fastened brilliant feathers to their bamboo earplugs. When the two were satisfied with their appearance, the party moved on. Everyone shouldered his pack once more, and they all marched in single file toward the village.

The village itself was a large, round commune, composed of adjoining shelters that opened onto a large open area. A steep, palm-leaf roof sloped from the center of the open area to the ground, forming both ceiling and outer wall for the families that lived side by side around the border. The entire structure was protected from enemy attack by a surrounding palisade of heavy poles.

One by one they followed their guides through a small opening between the poles, and crawled under a veil of leaves that hung loosely over the low entrance to the commune. With heads held high and eyes straight ahead, they paraded quickly past the startled villagers that swung in hammocks just inside the entrance.

The normal hum of activity erupted in shouts and cheers of welcome as the visitors marched briskly to the center of the clearing. Their hosts jumped to their feet in recognition of their arrival.

The men of the village had begun to move forward to greet their guests, when they suddenly realized that the unexpected party of visitors included not only four unknown Yanoamö, but also two tall fearsome strangers from the outside world. They hesitated for an instant but quickly gained control of the panic that had flashed across their faces. Then, while they continued to shout their greetings, they stepped backward and quietly reached for the bows and arrows they had left leaning against the framework of their shelters.

Dan and Paul stood silently in the center of the clearing with the rest of the visitors and assumed the formal, stoic stances that were traditional for visiting men. No trace of the nervousness inside showed on their faces while they watched their hosts get a firm grip on their weapons. Paul struggled to convince himself that it was all routine, but it was particularly unnerving to notice that a few of the men were tightening their bowstrings.

The tension diminished as the noise of their welcome subsided, but it never completely disappeared. The backpacks the men had carried into the village drew everyone's attention, and a crowd gathered to see how the contents would be distributed. When they realized that a large portion was destined for the big savannah, tempers flared. Why should they offer hospitality to people so brazen as to flaunt their possessions before them and then give them away to someone else?

As the afternoon wore on, the visitors were assigned two separate sleeping quarters. Three of the men who had accompanied Dana and Paul from the lowlands hung their hammocks with the two missionaries. The fourth, a young man named Chivirito, followed the two guides to a separate shelter on the opposite side of the village clearing.

The group had not been separated long before Chivirito returned to his companions. He found them engaged in animated conversation with some of their hosts, and he halted indecisively on the fringe of the crowd before he finally pushed his way forward to ask Dan for a paper and pencil. Dan ignored him for a moment, supposing that Chivirito only wanted to entertain his hosts with some trinkets from the outside world. But at Chivirito's nervous insistence, Dan finally opened one of the packs and handed over the items that had been requested.

Chivirito retreated a short distance, settled himself on a piece of firewood, and smoothed out the scrap of paper on his knee. Then, while a few Shamatali children watched with indifferent curiosity, he began the laborious task of forming the letters of a message he had just overheard.

He returned to the group a few moments later, squatted by Paul's hammock, and handed him the note. He waited patiently while his missionary friend scanned the message he had recorded, and he nodded almost imperceptibly when Paul raised his head to question Chivirito with his eyes. Then Paul turned back to the paper he held, and read it again.

"They're going to kill us for our backpacks."

The note was silently handed to Dan, and from there it was passed to the three other literates who had accompanied them. One by one they absorbed the message while the Shamatali men watched with amused interest. The Shamatali people had no concept of a message being shared via paper, nor any understanding of the literacy program that had taught their lowland kinsmen the mechanics of reading and writing.

There was no opportunity for private discussion. "Paul," Chivirito said, stretching as he stood, "hand me the gun. I'm going hunting." Paul hesitated a moment, wondering what was going on in Chivirito's mind––hoping he would not do anything rash.

"What are you going to shoot?" he asked, passing the shotgun to him.

"Wild turkeys," Chivirito replied with a blank expression. "I just need five shells."

Paul reached slowly for the ammunition box. Chivirito was obviously upset by the news he had overheard, and Paul was reluctant to provide ammunition for any well-intentioned heroism. Was he really going after wild turkeys? The four Yanoamö that accompanied them had all put their faith in Christ, but their old way of life was still fresh in their minds, and they were no strangers to the intrigue of a Yanoamö village.

At any rate, there was no way Paul could explain his hesitation without alerting the Shamatali men to the fact that their plot had been discovered; the only language they had in common was that of the Yanoamö.

The crowd around their hammocks had been following the conversation with practiced nonchalance. As Paul finally counted

Contact

five shells into Chivirito's hand, the Shamatali men laughingly wished him luck and told him to hurry back.

Pat Dye switched on the radio set and glanced anxiously at the clock. It was time for evening radio communication. Paul and Dan had wanted to conserve the battery of their portable two-way radio as much as possible, but Pat was sure Paul would call her on an evening as special as May 18. With a sudden burst of sentimentality, she hunted through a stack of records for a special favorite that was reminiscent of their wedding day six years earlier.

Suddenly the squawks and crackles of the radio were interrupted by her husband's voice, and Pat heard the call letters of the Tama Tama base. He had not forgotten! She hurried to the desk to acknowledge his call, but her smile vanished when the anniversary wishes she expected were replaced by an urgent prayer request.

"Honey," he said, "we're in the Shamatali village south of the big savannah, and the people are planning to kill us tonight. Pass the word and pray."

Radio sets in several missionary homes picked up the message. Paul was no alarmist, and his words were not taken lightly. Even while Dan and Paul were repacking their radio equipment in the darkness of the Shamatali village, their co-workers in the other locations were gathering together for prayer.

The men that had congregated around the hammocks of the outsiders finally sauntered off to the comfort of their own hearths. Dan and Paul were left alone with their three remaining companions, and were able at last to discuss their situation in low voices. Neither Pajarito nor the two younger men beside him seemed overly surprised to find themselves in such a predicament. They were strangely resigned to their fate. Their preoccupation centered more on a courageous death than on any attempt to escape. There *was* no escape.

Pajarito grimly wiped the blade of his machete and stuck it into the ground at his feet.

The five weary travelers were conscious of the fact that only the

Treasures of Darkness

Lord could intervene on their behalf. They encouraged one another with His goodness and power. They prayed. They sang. And when exhaustion overcame their personal concerns, they drifted into fitful sleep.

Campfires flickered in the darkness around the circle of the village clearing. A baby cried. A child coughed convulsively. Sporadic laughter rang out. And every so often a loud holler would break the stillness and awaken the sleeping visitors.

"Has he returned yet?"

Then the answer would come from the shelter where Chivirito was to have spent the night, "Not yet! He's still out with the gun!"

The sound of that dialogue repeated so often through the night chilled Dan and Paul to the bone. There was no mistaking the strategy of their hosts. All night long the hollering continued, and they realized, with a strange detachment, that once they were all together something was going to happen.

The village awoke with the first pale streaks of dawn, and Chivirito's hammock was still empty.

Paul hooked up the radio to let Pat know they had passed the night safely. Then while Dan and Pajarito searched the surrounding jungles for Chivirito, he and his two remaining companions tried to accommodate the large crowd that was collecting once more around their hammocks. Some wanted the trade goods that had been promised for food they had given the visitors the night before. Some tried once more to intimidate them into handing over their backpacks in their entirety. The two guides who had led them to the village came to collect their pay. This was as far as they were going.

Then out of the confusion a small, wiry man shuffled forward on his haunches and stopped in front of Paul's hammock. He grinned up into Paul's face, and his black eyes danced with excitement as he sized up the stranger before him. Paul smiled self-consciously. The man who studied him with such amusement seemed to be the perfect embodiment of every Yanoamö ideal. His red body bore the scars of warfare, and his face reflected cool self-confidence. He had not skimped on the wad of tobacco leaves he carried in his lower

Contact

lip, and the feather arm-bands that adorned his upper arms were just a little prettier than most.

After a moment's silence, Paul's new friend shifted his position and leaned forward to speak. "Outsider—do you want to go to the big savannah?"

Paul nodded, a little dumbfounded by the sudden answer to prayer. "Aren't you afraid to go there?" he asked the volunteer.

The man grinned at the ignorance of Paul's question. "I'm not a Shamatali," he laughed. "Why should *I* be afraid? I *live* on the big savannah. I just came here to visit some relatives!"

Dan and Pajarito returned with the news that they had found Chivirito but could not coax him to return to the village. He preferred to wait for them in the jungle.

An hour or so later they met him there and began the last leg of their journey. Paul chided him for deserting them the night before, and Chivirito explained his reasoning. He knew they would have no chance to defend themselves against so many people, but by waiting for his doom in the jungle he figured he would have a better chance of revenging his friends' deaths before he was killed. To him, the only dignity in death was the assurance that it would be properly avenged.

"That's why I asked you for the five shells," he explained. "I wanted to make sure you were all avenged before I died."

To Chivirito, such reasoning seemed perfectly logical. It was a matter of justice, not of conscience, and he did not consider it to be in conflict with his intention of following the Lord. And even though the missionaries tried once more to explain the concept that vengeance belongs to God, they were conscious of the fact that the Lord had used Chivirito's intentions, however doubtful, to save their lives.

The final stage of the journey took another day and a half. Their colorful guide, whom they eventually named José, took every opportunity to describe the warfare that raged on the big savannah. He delighted in telling of the men he had killed, and he grimly avowed his intention of adding to the list.

The four Yanoamö from the lowlands provided an appreciative

Treasures of Darkness

audience for his tales, but José found it mildly annoying that he could not stir an emotional response in the two outsiders. He paused in the middle of one such animated recital and studied Dan and Paul critically. They seemed far too complacent. Maybe he ought to make it a little more personal. "Do you realize you were nearly killed last night?" he grinned.

Dan and Paul rose a little in José's estimation when he discovered they not only had been aware of the plans, but also had relayed the news to others in the outside world. But he was not very impressed with their theory that it had been the Lord who had protected them.

"I'm the one who stopped them," he said. "I told them that if they killed you, we would avenge you ourselves. We want you on the big savannah."

José was no fool. People with access to knives, axes, fishhooks and machetes were more profitable alive than dead.

Wally and I learned the details of the contact weeks later when we returned from furlough with our four young children. The eldest was then nine years old, and the youngest was not yet a year old. We began making preparations to join Derek and Jill Hadley at the new location. An airstrip had been cleared on the savannah, the immunization program had been completed, and Paul and Dan had returned to the lowlands with their four Yanoamö companions.

We traveled to the Indian village where we had spent our first term with Joe and Millie Dawson while we adjusted to the language and culture of the Yanoamö. George and Fanny Radford, friends who were visiting from Canada, helped us pack the household necessities we had left in storage there. They would fly out to the big savannah with the children and me, and Wally would come on the next flight.

A sober group of Yanoamö friends watched us prepare the cargo for the flights that were to transport us and our equipment to the big savannah. They cautioned us to beware the sorcery and violence that were common among their unreached kinsmen. They warned us of the aggressiveness with which we would have to contend. And they wondered at the wisdom of taking clothing, dishes, and trade goods to people known to kill for material possessions. Some of them were not too sure we would ever meet again.

Their fears were not limited to the realm of the physical. The people of the big savannah had been shrouded in a veil of mystery for years, and in spite of our insistence to the contrary, there was still occasional speculation about whether they were entirely human.

At the time, it was easy to offer assurance that all would be well. The Lord majors in impossible situations. But a few months later I was to wonder whether my optimism had been based on faith in the Lord or ignorance of the problem.

2

The Big Savannah

To whom He was not spoken of, they shall see.

Romans 15:21

The plane dropped sharply into a winding valley, and the mountains rushed up to meet us. With a breathtaking change of scenery, the tropical jungle suddenly gave way to grassland, and a wide, rolling savannah spread out before us. I tingled with excitement. There it was at last–the big savannah of legendary fame, where Yanoamö life was said to have originated, and to where the spirits of the dead were said to return.

I smiled at the remembrance of the fantastic tales that were told concerning its people. The men were said to carry quivers designed with strange, supernatural zigzag patterns, and rumor had it that some had once been recognized as spirits of the dead. Many of the lowland people had set out on journeys to prove the truth of the story, but the way was long and rugged and the pilgrims had always turned back short of Yanoamö Paradise, as we laughingly called it. The group that had arrived with Dan and Paul was the first to complete the journey.

We caught a blurred glimpse of red bodies as we touched down on the grassy strip. People were streaming forth from the large, communal roundhouse on the far side of the savannah and racing toward the Hadleys' house, which was still under construction. They had already assembled in full splendor by the time we taxied to the clearing where Derek and Jill awaited us with their two little girls, Brenda and Marcia.

A tense crowd of naked warriors moved hesitantly toward us as the propeller spun to a stop. Their faces were smeared with black and purple paint, and their bodies glistened with oily, red dye. They showed a sudden burst of confidence as the plane stilled. Brandishing weapons and twanging their bowstrings, they converged on the little red Cessna in rowdy confusion.

Derek had told them that Wally would be arriving, and they did not realize that he had decided to wait for the second flight in deference to our visiting friends. When the children and I stepped to the ground with George and Fanny Radford, the men crowded around George shouting exuberant declarations of friendship while he tried in vain to exchange a few words of greeting with Derek. English made no sense to them and since their linguistic ability was limited to their own tribal language, they were thoroughly frustrated by George's lack of response. They shook Derek's arm impatiently. "Derico! DERICO! Stop talking and listen to us! Isn't this Wally? You said *Wally* was coming! Why doesn't he answer us?"

Derek and Jill, like us, had already learned a lowland version of Yanoamö and were able to carry on a conversation limited only by local dialect differences. Derek explained that Wally would be arriving on the next flight, and the spokesman for the welcoming committee pointed toward Fanny and me with his chin, asking if we were Wally's wives.

Fanny and I had been steering the children through the crowd toward Jill and the girls, but I could not resist stopping to answer for myself. I should have known better. As soon as I saw their startled expressions, and the delighted smiles that followed, I realized I had let my excitement carry me to a questionable extreme.

"Oh!" exclaimed the leader, promptly stepping toward us. "So you can speak our language!" His purple-streaked face broke into a wide grin as he planted himself firmly in front of us. He leaned his weight on the bow and arrows jabbed into the ground at his feet. "Well, you're certainly not bashful," he observed, leaning forward and grinning into my face so intently that I had to look somewhere else. "Are you really Wally's wife?"

"Yes, I am," I answered meekly, suddenly subdued as the men formed a tight circle around us. They barely exceeded five feet in stature, but their boldness gave them gigantic proportions. "And he's coming soon," I added, in a feeble gesture of self-defense. They burst into gales of laughter.

"Aren't you afraid to be here without your husband?" one of them queried with feigned concern. "Aren't you afraid of us?"

He shifted his position and moved a little closer. Obviously they thought I should have been, and by then I was not prepared to argue. I looked around frantically for Derek, but he was busy unloading cargo from the plane.

I grabbed Fanny's arm tightly, and told my inquisitors in what I hoped was a very annoyed tone of voice, that we wanted to talk with the *women*. We took a determined step forward, and they backed away.

We took refuge in the Hadleys' house, and I tried to regain my shattered composure. I had not been prepared for so aggressive a welcome, and it had been particularly unnerving to feel helpless before such a mob. "Paradise" was a little overwhelming. It wasn't only the Yanoamö who were delighted to see the plane return with Wally aboard.

The same boisterous crowd swarmed around the plane as Wally arrived, and their excitement grew as he stepped from the cabin. They surged around him in a tumult of shouts and laughter, waving their bows and arrows while they ceremoniously stomped a welcome for the visitors to the big savannah.

Smiling his acknowledgement of the fanfare, Wally had just begun to push his way toward us when a slight, muscular man blocked his path with an enthusiastic dance. Clasping an ax to his chest, he chanted in a loud monotone and pounded out a frenzied rhythm with his feet. His performance grew in intensity as the crowd cheered him on. Waving his ax above his head, he began to rattle off a string of phrases that drew a roar of laughter from the men around him.

The Big Savannah

His dance ended abruptly. Dropping his ax to the ground, he flung both arms around Wally's neck and hung there a moment in exhaustion. Then he studied the newcomer's face with laughing eyes. "Brother–" he panted, pausing to adjust the wad of tobacco leaves he held in his lower lip. "Could it be that you're really Wally?"

He pointed with his chin to Derek, still waiting to welcome Wally to the new base. "Derico over there told us your name is Wally. Is it?"

Wally laughingly admitted to his name, and his new friend hooted loudly and stomped his feet.

"And who are you?" Wally asked the dancer, sending a ripple of laughter through the crowd at the thought than anyone should be expected to tell his own name. But the dancer surprised them.

"I'm Jo–Jo–José," he sputtered, stumbling triumphantly over the strange new syllables of a Spanish name he was still learning to pronounce. "That's what Paul and Dan called me. You should say to me, 'Little One–José! Come and have something to eat!'"

He grinned up into Wally's face. Not everyone could boast a name he was unafraid to acknowledge!

Wally began to untangle himself from José's determined embrace. To the delight of the crowd, José began to stomp around again, still hugging the new arrival with one arm, and chanting all the while. "Hah! Hah! My brother has come to live with me! My brother has come to give me things! Axes to chop trees! Machetes to clear my garden! Clothing in which to dance! Hah!"

Wally finally pulled away, and the women on the fringe of the crowd backed off as he approached us, shielding their babies' faces so the sight of him would not scare them to death. They watched in awe as we exchanged enthusiastic hugs; then they huddled behind us and whispered their impressions of our excited conversation. Such gibberish we spoke! Could it be that we really understood each other?

Over the next two days, Paul Johnson, Missionary Aviation Fellowship pilot, continued to fly in with cargo. Little by little, the creaking shelves in the Hadleys' house and ours were stocked with

23

Treasures of Darkness

a three month supply of food, medicines, trade goods, and the building materials necessary to complete one house and begin another. Paul Dye and Dan Shaylor had offered us the little hut they had erected when they first arrived on the big savannah, and for the time being that had become our home, sweet home.

We quickly became acquainted with our rowdy neighbors. They surrounded us from dawn till dark, asking for things, arguing, shouting, and offering insistent advice on the best methods of building houses, washing clothes, repairing equipment, and training children. My vague dreams of teaching Bible stories to neat little rows of eager learners were fading fast.

We sat wearily around the campfire late one afternoon, roasting plantains over hot coals. The customary crowd pressed around us, and once the novelty of talking with the outsiders wore off, the conversation drifted toward the danger lurking in jungle shadows.

They were at war with an enemy village in the neighboring valley of Balafili, and they were soon absorbed in an intense discussion of the possibility of enemy attack.

One of them, a leader of the group, whose views on the subject seemed to be highly regarded, reached over his shoulder for the quiver that hung from his neck. He pulled it forward, carefully dumped new bamboo arrow points into his hand, and spread them out for inspection. But it was the quiver, not the points, that caught Wally's attention—especially the design that zigzagged the length of it.

Smiling in recollection of the lowland superstitions concerning the supernatural quivers of the big savannah, Wally asked to see it. He said he wanted to show it to George Radford.

With a nod of his head, the man on the opposite side of the campfire moved to hand over the quiver, hardly pausing in his grim description of how his new points could rip into a man. Then he suddenly realized that Wally had referred to George by name. He shook Wally's knee excitedly and asked with masked amusement that he say it again.

Wally complied, and they burst into laughter, asking the names of the rest of us, and repeating each one enthusiastically. They could not decide whether our willingness to reveal such personal things was due to great fearlessness or colossal ignorance. Our boldness both baffled and embarrassed them. Strong taboos forbade the telling of tribal names, especially among adult men, and they referred to one another either by terms of kinship or by village affiliation. Even though they knew we had no objection to the use of our names, they could hardly force themselves to speak with such audacity. They preferred to adopt us into the village and address us with terms of kinship. We were "Brother" and "Sister" to the younger generation and "Little One" to the older.

The leader who sat across from us clutching his zigzagged quiver leaned forward and caught Wally's attention. "Brother," he whispered confidentially, "I'm not afraid to tell my name either. I'm Timoteo. That's what Dan and Paul named me when they first arrived here."

He straightened up again and tried to appear indifferent to the admiration on the faces of his friends. If Timoteo had decided that Spanish names were not subject to tribal restrictions, that was good enough for them.

In the meantime, José arrived, dropped his bow and arrows to the ground, shoved some boys out of his way, and seated himself grandly by the fire. He warmed his hands and listened to the name game in progress. In spite of the fact that he, too, had been willing to divulge his own Spanish name, our freedom in saying our names still amused him. He studied Wally with mischievous eyes, and decided to try it himself.

Shuffling into a better position where he could face Wally at closer range, he took out his tobacco and laid it carefully on the top of his foot. "Brother," he began, spitting a stream of tobacco juice into the fire, "what's your son's name?"

Bobby fidgeted under the amused gaze of so many eyes suddenly focused on him.

"Bobby."

"Bobby!" José laughed. "Dear old Bobby! Hah!"

He was delighted that it worked so easily. He nodded to Janice, busily fanning the fire, and was about to ask her name when the others coached him in a loud whisper, suggesting he ask about the bigger one. He grinned his appreciation of their help. He had not realized there was an older one in the house.

"Brother, what do you call your older daughter?"

"Lynne."

"Lynne! Dear old Lynne! My own little Lynne!"

José enjoyed being the center of attention, and he waxed bolder with all the encouragement he received from some of the more timid ones around him. "And is Lynne old enough to be married?"

The snickers that accompanied his remark left little doubt that the line of questioning was moving beyond the acceptable. Child brides were common to the Yanoamö marriage customs, but apparently José's remarks were not considered to be entirely innocent.

The laughter faded to a heavy, uncomfortable silence as Wally responded to José's grin with a cool appraisal that soon had everyone fidgeting.

"Don't say that to me," Wally answered evenly. "Don't ever make suggestions involving my daughters. If anyone were to bother my girls," he said, with a deliberate pause, "I'd really be angry."

It was an ambiguous statement, and one that Wally hoped he would never have to define. But it seemed to have the desired effect.

His words hung in the air for an agonizing moment before José broke the stillness by jerking his head to one side in annoyance. He pressed a clenched fist to his mouth and swayed from side to side. Someone whispered nervously that Wally had made him angry.

Then José turned with a quick switch of emotion and put an arm around Wally's shoulders. "Brother," he smiled, "I'm just talking that way so we can laugh. Don't be upset." He leaned closer to study Wally's face. "Do you outsiders really protect your women?"

"Of course they do," the others answered impatiently, anxious to make amends. "They're just like us."

They glanced at one another uneasily, hunched around the fire, and some began to shift their weight and clear their throats. Timoteo shuffled forward and put a firm hand on Wally's shoulder.

The Big Savannah

"Brother," he nodded soberly, "we defend *our* women, too. We fight for them." He paused a moment to let the full significance sink in.

"Right now our women are afraid of you," he continued.

Wally nodded.

"*Should* they be afraid?" Timoteo asked.

"I wouldn't touch them."

"No, maybe not," Timoteo agreed, glancing quickly toward the other men to make sure they were listening. "But it is best they stay afraid anyhow."

The conversation was over, and the group around the fire looked at one another with evident relief as they gathered their bows and arrows together and prepared to leave. The sun had disappeared behind the mountains, and the barricade surrounding the village would soon be shut for the night.

The following morning Timoteo was annoyed to hear the laughter of women as he passed our house, and he burst through the door to investigate the commotion.

To us, he was just one of many who constantly tried to intimidate us with threats and demands, and we did not realize the authority his voice carried. He did not expect his word to be taken lightly.

He glared at the women, scattering them with a glance, and then turned to Wally. He had not found any cause for complaint, but the anger he had felt at finding our house full of women was still there. "Give me some fishhooks," he said, in an attempt to justify his presence.

"What do you have to trade?" Wally asked. "Bananas?"

"Nothing," Timoteo snapped, eyeing Wally with animosity and shifting his weight impatiently from one foot to the other.

"You can't have them for nothing," Wally said. "Do you want to work?"

"No. Just give me one, then, if you're going to be so stingy."

The women, huddled in the corner, were nodding vigorous encouragement to Wally, but he was not prepared to be intimidated. He shook his head. Timoteo stormed all the louder,

Treasures of Darkness

and Wally finally turned his back on him.

"Are you deaf?" Timoteo screamed, twanging his bowstring angrily. "Can't you *hear* me, outsider?"

Wally ignored him, and Timoteo grabbed for one of the arrows he had left beside the door. He slipped it quickly into position and drew the bowstring back to his ear. His face was dark with rage, and every muscle in his body seemed taut with emotion.

My heart beat wildly. I looked to Wally for reassurance, but his face was a blank. The only emotion that showed was a determination to set precedents we would be able to live with.

"Outsider!" Timoteo bellowed, infuriated by the fact that Wally would not even acknowledge his threats. "I'll shoot you! I'll make your blood flow!"

He held the quivering arrow on Wally for an endless moment, then suddenly withdrew it. He slapped it angrily against his bow, and stomped out of the house hurling loud insults over his shoulder.

For a moment the house was silent. Then the women that had watched the episode giggled with relief and crowded around their new hero. "My dear older brother!" exclaimed one of the most ardent. "Don't you fear *anyone*?" She reached up and wrapped her arms around his neck, smiling into his surprised face. She was promptly unwrapped and scolded, and Wally escaped to the Hadleys' house.

The next day the plane arrived with our final load of supplies, and the Radfords prepared for their flight back to civilization. A crowd gathered around the plane to bid them a customary farewell, promising to cry faithfully for them if they would just leave some small remembrance behind. They clamored for Fanny's dress, pestered George to sharpen their machetes just once more, begged for a suitcase, and pleaded for a necklace.

Timoteo strode to the plane with a set of bow and arrows he wanted to send with George. He spoke with cool self-confidence that defied mention of his violent outburst the day before.

There were no trade goods handy, but sensing that his offer to trade comprised an apology, George began unbuttoning his shirt.

The Big Savannah

Timoteo grinned broadly, and the crowd around the plane cheered the outsider who was willing to take the shirt off his back in order to reach an agreeable exchange.

The passengers were finally strapped into their seats, and the propeller whirred into action, creating a gust of wind that blew grass and dust into the faces of everyone behind the plane. The crowd scrambled to safer vantage points to watch the takeoff. We waved our final good-byes and watched the plane taxi to the end of the runway. Soon it was speeding past our house and lifting into the air.

The people milling around us laughed and shouted as the plane gained altitude and headed toward the mountains. They had enjoyed the excitement of the past few days and the adventure of helping carry mysterious boxes from the pod of the plane to the outsiders' houses. It was over now, and it mattered not at all to them that three moons would die before the plane returned.

But there was little excitement in the hearts of four, lone outsiders standing by the airstrip like small, insignificant dots on the big savannah. We followed the tiny speck with our eyes until it disappeared between the mountains; then we turned back to our houses with a strange, unsettling loneliness. For a few days the little Cessna had served as a link with civilization, but now it was gone, and we were acutely aware of the distance that separated us from all that was familiar. We may have been heroes in the eyes of the churches that had cheered us on our way, but to the people around us we were ignorant, tongue-tied strangers with no apparent usefulness.

Days of adjustment began as we familiarized ourselves with our new surroundings and worked out practical solutions to the problems that confronted us. Derek and Wally set themselves to complete the basic housing requirements as quickly as possible, in order to devote themselves entirely to the Yanoamö.

In the meantime, we would adjust to the new dialect of the language we had learned in the lowlands, establish a rapport with the volatile personalities around us, and whet their appetite to spiritual concepts.

Treasures of Darkness

Wally spent a good part of each day helping Derek get his house completed so they could begin work on a permanent home for us. While he was away, the children and I entertained a steady stream of visitors who tested the limits of our endurance and attempted to determine our status in the village.

I was always on guard against frequent attempts by our guests to sneak out of the house with crayons, safety pins, spoons, and books that had been left on the floor by our two youngest children, Janice and Davey. Whenever I caught someone trying to escape with something, they would cheerfully return it and sit back down on the floor to await the next opportunity.

Stealing articles of obvious value was frowned on, but to run off with something that had been found on the floor was considered more a game than a crime. If I caught them before they were out the door, *I* won. If they managed to smuggle it successfully into their own house, *they* won, and I was not supposed to ask for its return. That was where our opinions often clashed.

Arguments over stolen articles were totally exhausting. Our new friends suffered no inhibition against losing their tempers, and our attempts to retrieve our possessions usually resulted in a volley of shouts and threats that left us limp.

In an attempt to avoid such conflicts, I began taking my work outside as much as possible and entertaining visitors around the campfire. In spite of the fact that a small propane gas stove had been flown in for us, we continued using an outdoor fire for boiling the daily drinking water. We were able to conserve fuel that way, and the flames of the fire provided a warmth and atmosphere our guests enjoyed.

Out by the campfire, I would wash my clothes in pails of water, and the women would giddily experiment with the soap, lathering their children and tossing them into the stream. Apart from the fact that a few laundry enthusiasts often left indelible red fingerprints on the diapers, the arrangement seemed quite satisfactory. But I could not always manage to keep an eye on the door of the house.

We were absorbed in an impromptu discussion of creation one

The Big Savannah

afternoon, when a little boy grabbed me urgently by the arm, and told me that Wishiquimi had stolen some food. We all rushed to the house and examined a stack of fresh corn I had just received in exchange for some thread.

"He's right!" everyone began to yell. "It's not all here!"

They began loud condemnations of Wishiquimi–whoever that was–making good use of her name as they did so. I grabbed a pencil and scribbled it down for future reference. We had not figured out the limitations of the taboos concerning names, but they seemed to think she did not deserve to have her name protected right then.

"Call Wally! Call Derek!" they shouted at me impatiently. "Run after her!"

I hesitated to admit that I did not know who she was, and asked instead where she had been sitting. "Don't you remember? She was right on this log beside you, holding her baby girl!" I pulled out the paper and added a notation that Wishiquimi had a little daughter. We would need all the clues we could get. But I balked at their suggestion that I set off in hot pursuit. The rest of the corn would probably disappear while I was gone.

The following morning we locked the doors and set out for the village, four or five minutes' walk across the savannah. We were going to do our best to salvage our corn and our honor.

Down the trail and across the swamp we marched, stepping carefully over the garbage heaps that surrounded the village, until we arrived at the barricade of poles that enclosed the roundhouse. We climbed through a small daytime opening, stepped gingerly across some poles that spanned a filthy mud-hole, and stopped uncertainly at the edge of the village clearing.

Scrawny, snarling dogs ran at us from all sides, and a stick of firewood was hurled at them from a nearby shelter. We studied the wide circle of "houses" built side by side around the village clearing and wondered where to begin. There were more than two hundred people in the village, and none of us was even sure whom it was we were looking for.

We ducked under a row of long palm leaves that formed the

front wall of the closest shelter. People swung in hammocks strung in triangle formation around smoky campfires and offered us sticks of firewood to sit on. The sides of each adjoining house were open, so that all the shelters seemed to run together in one long, continuous hallway of hammocks and campfires. Baskets, gourds, and neatly wrapped bundles hung from the roofs, and a good supply of firewood was stacked under the eaves.

The occupants of the adjoining shelters made their way over the tangle of intervening hammocks and joined the crowd around us. They asked the purpose of our visit, and when we mentioned Wishiquimi by name, there was a moment of startled silence. Then they howled with laughter.

They could not figure out how we had ever come to discover her tribal name, but they were absolutely delighted with the casual way we used it. It would not have been so funny if we had been naming any of *them*.

"Who did you say stole your corn?" they would laugh, motioning one another to silence. "Who was it?"

We made our way around the circle of shelters, answering the same questions at every stop and providing the villagers with an hour's entertainment that they thoroughly enjoyed. We tried to conceal the fact that we would not have recognized our illustrious corn thief had we been speaking with her face to face.

Our investigation came to a sudden close when José's brother ran into the clearing with the breathless announcement that men from a nearby village had broken into our house and stolen some of our clothing.

The following day, Derek and Wally set out for the little village nestled in the jungle on the opposite side of the savannah, about forty-five minutes' walk away. The stolen articles did not represent a significant financial outlay, but there was more at stake than dollars and cents. Carelessness in retrieving our personal belongings would have triggered a wave of thievery we never could have coped with, and we would have quickly lost not only the remainder of our possessions but also the respect we hoped to gain.

A grim crowd of well-wishers lingered in front of our house and watched Derek and Wally as they disappeared down the valley. They may have found Wishiquimi's escapade amusing, but there was no hint of a smile as they denounced the scoundrels from the neighboring village. They were much more indulgent with themselves than they were with others.

The men looked at me soberly before they headed back to the roundhouse. "There's going to be a fight," they predicted. "They won't get anything back without a fight."

The women crowded around me silently, as though to cushion the shock. They pouted, blinked a few tears from their eyes, and squeezed my arm tightly in a gesture of consolation. Then they followed me into the house, where I sat in a quandary, wondering whether the situation really did warrant more concern than I actually felt.

A young couple with family ties in both villages accompanied Derek and Wally over the hills. As they neared their destination, the girl raced ahead to warn the villagers of their coming. Her husband, equally nervous concerning the welfare of both sides, tried to arm Derek and Wally with clubs, but they refused. At that stage, they were not sure if the poles he offered were supposed to give them a manly image, or if they were supposed to fight with them, or if they were simply to be used later as "exhibit A" in a self-defense plea by the villagers tensely awaiting their arrival.

The village was deathly still as they approached. The girl who had run ahead of Derek and Wally had sounded the alarm, and the village had prepared for a major attack. Who knew what to expect of two angry outsiders?

Derek and Wally squeezed through the opening of the palisade and ducked under the leaves that hung over the entrance of the village. The moment they stepped into the clearing, a great confusion of noise erupted. With a wild shout, a line of warriors rushed across the clearing and surrounded them with arrows drawn.

In the background, guards posted at each family section

stomped the ground and shouted their encouragement to one another. The air was filled with bows and arrows, clubs, axes, and machetes. Children screamed, dogs barked, and a woman wailed in fear as the outsiders hesitated a moment and then stepped forward.

Deciding there was no alternative but to go ahead with their investigation, Derek and Wally stepped into the prearranged plan of searching the village. They barged into the first shelter so quickly that the guard had to withdraw his arrow in order to prevent a collision. Baffled by the fact that the outsiders showed no interest in a physical confrontation, the angry crowd that had surrounded them in the clearing followed behind and continued a verbal barrage.

From shelter to shelter, Derek and Wally circled the village, methodically dumping the contents of every basket onto the ground amid a din of threats and curses, demanding the return of their clothing. They were careful to avoid any personal contact that might be construed as aggression.

The circuit was completed and nothing was found, but they were positive the clothing was there somewhere. The guilt of the village was obvious in the tension that threatened to explode at any moment.

Deciding to adopt a more culturally acceptable method of solving the problem, Derek and Wally marched determinedly into the center of the village clearing. They planted their feet firmly apart, squared their shoulders, and began to sway slightly from side to side in sober imitation of the way they had often seen Timoteo and José demonstrate their displeasure. They cleared their throats impressively, and both began to speak at once.

With all the animation they could muster, Derek and Wally launched into a bold attack, chanting their complaints in typical Yanoamö style. The tumult around them began to fade, and the warriors who still encircled them began to glance uneasily at one another.

An old man hurried forward to calm the outsiders with assurances that no one had taken anything, but his anxiety over

The Big Savannah

their newly designed accusations served only to convince them that their charges were finally being taken to heart. Ignoring his pleas for silence, they carried on louder than ever, adding a complaint against the inhospitable reception they had just received when they came to request the return of their clothing.

The old man began to holler at the women and children who were watching the excitement from the safety of their shelters. "Go and get this man's things! Right now! Hurry up! Bring me everything you took!"

Derek and Wally were delighted with the sudden turn of events, and continued their performance with renewed enthusiasm, echoing the old man's instructions to the women and the children.

A group of boys hurried from the village and soon retuned with a pile of clothing they soberly placed in the old man's hands. He handed them to Derek and Wally piece by piece. Their victory was so surprising that they had a little difficulty maintaining their annoyance, but they persevered, examining each article that was returned and loudly protesting every smudge and stain. Their arms were soon draped with more clothing than we had realized was missing.

Jill and I were still in the dark, anxiously watching the clock. Each of us was on guard duty in our own home, about a minute's walk apart. We could not be of any mutual encouragement, and the gloomy predictions we had heard earlier were reinforced by the solemn groups of women who gathered sympathetically around each of us in our separate homes.

"Sister," one of my comforters whispered to me, "would you cry if your man were hurt?" I supposed I would. They whispered among themselves for a moment.

"Who's going to carry Bobby's father home?" asked another. "What if he's just lying somewhere?"

I did not answer immediately, so she leaned forward to whisper another question. "Sister, do you outsiders die?"

They whiled away the time with anxious whispers, sharing the gory details of their thoughts concerning the fight on the other side of the savannah. They were a sober group for a change, and it

Treasures of Darkness

chilled me to realize that their opinions reflected an inside view of normal Yanoamö behavior. Maybe Wally and Derek were really in danger. I tried to shut my mind to the possibility.

I stood in the doorway and searched the long, empty valley. The women watched me wistfully, wishing I would release the tears they felt sure I was hiding. "Sister," one of them whispered. "Come sit with us here. We'll cry with you."

Their own eyes brimmed with tears, and they nodded their encouragement for me to join them. They shifted their position to make a little more room on the dirt floor, but I declined. I shook my head and returned to my bench beside the table.

My uneasiness was growing, but I was afraid to stop hoping that everything was all right. Reaching for a Bible, I thumbed through the book of Isaiah, scanning the pages for a comforting word. My eyes caught the word *weapon*, and I stopped. Nothing could have sounded more appropriate. I read and reread Isaiah 54:17, "*No weapon that is formed against thee shall prosper . . . this is the heritage of the servants of the Lord.*"

I struggled inwardly for a moment, realizing that if such a verse were really an all-occasion promise, there would be no such thing as martyrdom. But finally deciding that if God had intended to prepare my heart for bad news He would have chosen a different verse, I accepted it at face value and got up to prepare supper.

The women noticed my change of attitude and asked why my sorrow had gone away. "Why should I be afraid?" I replied with new confidence. "The paper says God will protect them. The men over there can't hurt them."

"Hoh," they answered, looking blankly at one another. A moment passed and one of them got to her feet.

"I'm going home," she announced. "If we're not going to cry there's no use sitting here and doing nothing." The others got to their feet and followed her out the door, puzzled at the message I had received.

Derek and Wally arrived soon after, smiling broadly while they recounted their adventures. Not only had they left on good terms with the neighboring village, but the men who had threatened their

The Big Savannah

lives were so anxious to convince them that there were no hard feelings that they invited us all over for a visit.

The following morning, a woman who had invited me to call her "Mother" arrived at the door in great agitation. She did not look at me as she spoke, but since I was the only one around, it seemed fairly obvious that the tirade was directed at me.

"Always calling people's names!" she shouted. "Always using my daughter's name! Why do you act like an enemy?"

I stared at her with bewilderment.

"Why are you treating my daughter this way?" she continued. "She's so frightened she can't even eat!"

The light finally dawned. "Are you Wishiquimi's mother?" I asked incredulously.

She nodded with annoyance, jerking her head angrily as I repeated the offense. Would I *never* learn how insulting it was to use proper names? "Are you going to hurt her?" she asked. "What are you going to do?"

I said I was only going to ask for my corn back, and she laughed with relief. She squeezed onto the bench beside me and smiled condescendingly.

"Little One, your corn was no good. It was old and tough. You would not have liked it anyway. Why are you so angry?" She was suddenly all love and tenderness. She hugged me impetuously, and I had difficulty retaining my disapproval.

"So *you* ate my corn!" I scolded. She put a calming hand on my shoulder, but I refused to be unruffled. "If you and your daughter have already eaten it, you will have to pay for it in bananas."

She laughingly agreed, and later returned with a stalk of stubby little *fatulima* that I was too ignorant to recognize as the lowest form of banana life available.

The next time she came, she was accompanied by a young woman carrying a baby girl. It *had* to be Wishiquimi. She looked so nervous that I avoided mention of the subject for a while.

Finally my curiosity prompted me to test her reaction. "I'm not angry at you," I said, in a gallant offer to forgive and forget.

She nodded and smiled disarmingly. *Why should you be angry?*

She seemed to say.

I decided to use a more direct approach. "Don't steal from me again. I get annoyed when people take my food."

She studied my face with puzzled, innocent eyes. "*I've* never stolen from you," she assured me. "*I* didn't take your corn. Other people steal but *I* don't."

A loud clattering awakened us as José's brother, Julio, banged impatiently on the side of the house. "Brother! Wally! Are you still sleeping?" he shouted. He jabbed an arrow through a crack in the wall to attract our attention. "Brother! Hurry! Get up and light the fire! I'm cold!"

Wally sighed with resignation and reached for his clothes. He climbed down the ladder from the loft, where we slept on a scattering of foam mats, and groped his way across the dirt floor in the semidarkness. He fumbled with the lock and opened the door to his friend.

Julio hurried in shivering, and squatted on the floor. He had been drenched in a cold, rainy-season drizzle. He hugged himself contentedly while Wally hunted for the matches, and let his eyes wander over the luxury of the rough little hut that had become our temporary home.

His early-morning visits were becoming part of the daily routine. He liked to call in on his way home from predawn hunting trips to let us know whether his venture had been successful.

"I didn't see anything at all this morning," he sighed. "Everything was frighteningly still. There must be raiders around."

Wally found the matches and followed Julio outside into the chilly morning fog to start the campfire. He gazed absently into the jungle behind the house and wondered whether a party of enemy warriors could really be hiding in the shadows.

We had heard of Julio long before we had been able to identify him personally. Derek had often spoken of him, sharing information he had gleaned before our arrival. In fact, the fear of enemy attack was due to the death of two men killed by Julio and his cousin. A war party from the Balafili valley had attacked the

The Big Savannah

people on the big savannah to avenge a death they attributed to witchcraft. Two men had been injured in the skirmish, and when the attacking village fled, Julio and his cousin had pursued them. They had overtaken them in the jungles and killed two of them, plunging their family and friends into an icy era of fear as they awaited the inevitable retaliation.

Julio scraped together the charred remains of a previous fire, added a few dry twigs, and held a match to the kindling. He coaxed the flame with soft clicking noises, and he and Wally were soon huddled over the crackling warmth of a new fire.

Julio took a deep breath and drew in his stomach, giving it a solid, resounding smack to show how empty he was. He sighed and shuffled closer to the fire. "Brother," he said, "if we had more food we'd really feed you well. But we're hungry ourselves these days."

His face hardened in anger as he surveyed the nearby jungles. "There are raiders all over the place," he said, with a bitterness that ignored his own responsibility for the present dilemma. "We can't even walk safely to the garden."

Wally nodded his understanding and assured Julio that we had brought plenty of food with us.

"Brother," Julio began again, studying Wally's face across the flames, "do you know our enemies?"

He reached out his hand and grasped Wally by the shoulder. "Do you know them?" he repeated. "Do you care about what's happening? Would you shoot them if you saw them?"

The answer was difficult to form into words. Wally knew he would be misunderstood. He *did* care. But he cared about the enemy village too.

Wally shook his head. "No," he answered, after a difficult pause. "I can't shoot them. My gun is just for wild game."

They gazed at one another for a moment, and then Julio withdrew his hand. He turned away in disgust. "No. Don't help us," he muttered sarcastically. "Don't defend us. Just let them kill us. It doesn't matter."

The two of them sat in silence for a while. "We didn't come to kill people," Wally said, in a halting explanation of our objectives.

"We came to share a message of life, not of death. The witchcraft and warfare could be ended if you people knew the Lord."

Julio was not impressed. He knew that it would take more than a strange message from the outside world to convince the enemy village to lay down their arms.

Wally stayed by the campfire long after Julio had gone, reflecting on the conversation. Julio was not the only one who had been disgusted lately with our determined neutrality. Many shared his disillusionment with the unreasonable limitations of our friendship. The rapport we had hoped to establish with the people seemed a long way off, and apart from involving ourselves in their welfare, there seemed to be nothing we could do about it.

The days passed, and the women who enjoyed afternoon visits around our campfire decided that our impartiality must be based more on ignorance than on any personal affection for the enemy village. They set themselves to the task of enlightening me, but their patience was sorely tried.

They wandered up the trail toward our house one afternoon and broke into a run as they spied me beside the campfire. Yelling my name enthusiastically, baskets bouncing on their backs, they hurried toward me. Laughing and hollering, they pushed one another in frenzied attempts to see who could reach me first.

They dropped their baskets to the ground and flung themselves at me from every direction. I loved their rowdy visits as much as they did and cheerfully set aside my soap and laundry pails while they squeezed into every available inch of space around the fire.

They hung their arms around my neck, draped their legs over my knees, and showered me with enthusiastic invitations to accompany them on a tadpole-hunting expedition. I declined, making vague promises for some other day, and explained that I had to finish washing the clothes.

"At the river?" they asked soberly. Realizing those were my intentions, they decided someone had better stay with me. "You shouldn't go to the stream alone," they scolded, as they had often done before. "Don't you know that when raiders are around you shouldn't go *near* the jungle?"

The Big Savannah

Their constant warnings made me uneasy, but having never decided whether their preoccupation with raiders was exaggerated or realistic, I had not really taken them very seriously. The trouble was that their humor was always too close to the surface. Many a lengthy discourse had been interrupted by great bursts of laughter over some ignorant comment of mine, and the seriousness of the situation had been lost. I never knew where the reality ended and the joke began.

Three women decided to stay behind and protect me. When we were ready to move our laundering operations to the stream, some twenty yards behind the house, they reluctantly accompanied me to stand guard while I rinsed the clothes.

Carefully searching the shadows on the opposite bank, they climbed down to the water's edge and helped me down beside them. Two of them swished into the stream to hunt for crabs, and the third sat beside me at the edge of the water, hugging her knees and moaning predictions of doom.

Among ourselves, we had come to refer to them as Crooked Tooth, Laughing Lady, and Laughing Lady's Fat Daughter—a vivacious girl admired by women and sought after by men because of her plump physique. It was Laughing Lady who sat beside me in morbid discontent, whispering a tearful account of the warfare as she scanned the jungle on the opposite shore for any unusual movement.

"They were angry over a man's death," she pouted. "And they blamed us for doing witchcraft. It was not us at all. We told them it must have been the Shamatali people who had done it, but they wouldn't listen."

She paused a moment, humming plaintively as she recalled the painful details. Smearing a tear across her cheek, she sat quietly for a moment. Then a distant hooting in the jungle froze everyone in their tracks.

Laughing Lady jumped to her feet, and the women in the stream scrambled frantically to the bank. Crooked Tooth and Laughing Lady's Fat Daughter grabbed their baskets and followed Laughing Lady up the steep incline, hollering for me to follow. They were half laughing and half crying as they scurried up the slope, slipping and sliding on wet feet, and yelling at one another to move faster. Panting and giggling, they ran to the house, dropped their baskets to the ground, and looked around for me.

"Margarita!" they shouted, laughing in surprise as they realized I had not followed them. "Sister! Aren't you coming?"

Their hilarity had convinced me that nothing was seriously wrong, but before I had time to consider an answer, Laughing Lady's Fat Daughter made a mad dash back to the stream to save me. She slid down the bank and grabbed me by the wrist. Holding me tenaciously with one hand, and reaching for my pail of wet laundry with the other, she managed to drag me up the bank to safety. Then she collapsed in laughter and entertained the other two with a colorful account of how she had found me still rinsing clothes in the stream.

It was not until I saw the brutality of tribal warfare a few months later that I fully appreciated the risk she had taken in running back to my rescue.

The woods were alive with shouts. The call we had first heard at the stream had been relayed all the way to the village, alerting the men to the fact that raiders had been spotted. Warriors poured forth from every exit of the roundhouse and raced down the path with bows and arrows, hooting their encouragement to one another. Men, women, and children followed behind screaming for blood.

The party paused for a moment beside our house while the men in charge decided which trail each one should take. Some were grimly intent on the business at hand, and others were dashing about with an excitement that seemed more befitting a stadium than a battlefield. Once their courses had been plotted, they disappeared into the jungles, and we could hear them calling back and forth to keep track of each other as the search for raiders began.

I was thoroughly confused about whether the danger was real. Did they honestly believe there were enemies hiding in ambush nearby, or were they just practicing their war tactics? But I was no more baffled by their reactions than they were by mine. They could not fathom my reluctance to acknowledge the fact that someone had discovered a raiding party just downstream from our house.

The men retuned a while later announcing that they had chased the raiders away.

"Did you really see them?" I asked, a little incredulously.

"No, but we saw their tracks."

"Maybe your own people made those tracks."

They studied me for a moment, wondering at the level of my mentality, then shrugged their shoulders and walked away.

The women stayed by the house and gathered around the fire, asking why we outsiders never feared the raiders. Was it because God had already made us eternal and we knew we were indestructible? I hesitated to tell them that our fearlessness was based on an assumption that a good many of their raider alarms were false. I realized they could not afford to make such presumptions.

Laughing Lady began to rehearse our escapade at the river for the benefit of those who had not been around to enjoy the show. "But why were you so frightened?" I asked. "Raiders would not kill women anyway, would they?"

Laughing Lady's Fat Daughter shook me impatiently by the arm. "Margarita," she said, grabbing a sharp stick to mock an attack on me, "when the raiders hide by the trail they let us come close, then jab us like this!" She emphasized her point with a poke at my leg. I drew in my breath sharply, and Laughing Lady erupted in laughter until the tears rolled down her cheeks.

"Little One," she said, as the hilarity subsided, "raiders are *dangerous*. They want to shoot the men, but if they're angry enough they will kill anybody. They would even strangle little children."

The group was suddenly serious again. Laughing Lady leaned forward and touched my arm lightly. "Little One," she added, "don't be deceived. They would even strangle *your* children."

After a moment's silent reflection, they began to stretch to their feet. It was getting late, and they still had to collect firewood for the

Treasures of Darkness

night. At least they now had the assurance that there were no raiders hidden along the trail.

In the days that followed, raider alarms began to occur with unnerving regularity, and we were bombarded with desperate appeals for help. The effectiveness of Wally's shotgun had been proven on hunting trips, and our neighbors tried every tactic to draw him into the warfare. They pleaded, they argued, they threatened, but it was to no avail.

Constant fear of ambush took its toll in frayed nerves and frequent squabbles. Gardening and hunting were unattended, and hunger pangs added to the general misery. The village leaders finally decided to evacuate the village for a few days. Small family groups scattered in the distant jungles would be able to enjoy a reprieve beyond the normal reach of raiders.

They prepared us for our lonely vigil by painting vivid pictures of evils that might befall us in their absence. We took their warnings lightly, so they tried all the more to persuade us of the danger we faced, embellishing their stories with blood and violence. We did not need to expect any special treatment from the enemy warriors just because we were outsiders.

Some seemed genuinely concerned for our welfare, but there was something sinister in the warnings of the others. They would have felt a little more rewarded for their efforts if they had realized how uneasy I was becoming. The prophecies that we would all be killed for our possessions were so many that I began to wonder if they were not just trying to shift the blame in advance for something they intended to do themselves. Would they really harm us? The farewell warnings we had received from the lowland Yanoamö when we had prepared for our first trip to the big savannah flooded my mind.

We visited the village a day or so before their planned departure. There were indications of warfare everywhere. Long green arrow shafts that had been carried home from nearby gardens leaned against the houses to dry in the sun. Inside the shelters, small groups of men huddled around smoky fires, tying feathers on new shafts and appraising the potency of new, poison-tipped arrow

The Big Savannah

points.

A man in a blue striped shirt bent over the yellowing shaft he was drying over hot ashes. He picked it up and tested its weight with a practiced hand. Holding it in shooting position, he ran his eye quickly down the length of it, twirling it to check for curvature. Satisfied with its reliability, he laid it across his knees and paused to talk with us a while.

He was a man in his early thirties whom Derek had recently named Enrique. He appeared to be part of the loosely organized hierarchy of the village, and though he shared neither José's rough aggressiveness nor Timoteo's passion for violence, his word seemed to carry authority in a large section of the village. Enrique's preoccupation was more for the welfare of his friends than for the destruction of his enemies. He lacked no skill as a warrior, but the power he really preferred was that of the spirit world. Perhaps it was that very interest in the supernatural that gave him a unique desire to hear about the God we knew.

"Tell me more about God," he grinned, relaxing in his hammock. "Is He friendly?" A few of Enrique's brothers joined us, and squatted beside Derek and Wally around the campfire.

"Yes, He's friendly." Derek began, groping for the right words to explain God's concern for the Yanoamö. "He's the one who makes your plantains grow. And He made the armadillo and the tapir—"

"And people," Enrique interrupted, nodding as he recalled what he had heard us say before. "He likes people, doesn't He? People like us?"

Derek nodded. "If He didn't, He wouldn't bother warning us about hell. He really wants to save us from destruction."

The crowd around the fire leaned forward to make sure they would not miss any details as Derek repeated the Gospel story. They nodded their understanding and smiled in appreciation of the happy ending that was promised. They all began to talk at once.

"Tell Him we *do* like His Son," they grinned, shaking Derek and Wally by the arm. "Tell Him we want Him to protect us."

"*You* tell Him!" Derek laughed, "He understands your language!" Enrique grinned, as he always did at that suggestion.

Treasures of Darkness

"Little One," an old man said, grabbing Wally's arm, "have you really seen God? Is His appearance frightening?"

"I haven't seen His face," Wally began hesitantly. "But I know Him inside." He paused a moment, wondering how such a theological mystery could be explained.

"Yes, yes, yes," Enrique smiled, slapping himself on the chest. "I know what you mean. It's the same with the spirits. You don't see them with your eyes, but they live inside, and you know they're there."

He sat upright in his hammock, drew a deep breath, and clapped his hands together, meaning that it was time to get back to work. "The raiders may be close," he smiled, excusing himself from further conversation. He stooped over the fire once more and continued to dry his arrow shaft.

We walked around the circle of the village with the Hadleys, pausing for brief visits here and there, and pondering Enrique's interest in the Gospel. Formal meetings had not yet been started, because of the building program still in progress, but a steady stream of visitors from dawn till dark had given all of us many opportunities for sharing the Word. Did Enrique only seek protection from the raiders he feared, or was he really starting to understand the eternal values of which we had often spoken?

Morning fog still blanketed the airstrip when the exodus began. The women walked slowly, bent under heavily laden baskets containing all of their earthly goods. Small babies in rough bark slings bounced at the women's hips, and toddlers too young to keep up with the rest perched on top of the baskets and wrapped their arms tightly around their mothers' heads. Older children and scrawny dogs walked beside them, and the crippled and the maimed trailed behind. A few men, well-armed with bows and arrows, guarded each family unit as the procession moved slowly across the savannah and disappeared into the jungles.

An hour later we were alone. How quiet the world seemed! The Hadleys joined us for a leisurely cup of coffee, but we could not relax. The eerie stillness was too distracting, and we had forgotten how to enjoy our privacy.

The Big Savannah

We had not been alone for long before word spread to the surrounding villages that the people on the big savannah had taken up temporary residence in the jungles. The first to take advantage of the situation were the people from the nearby village where Derek and Wally had made their dramatic recovery of stolen clothing. A friendship had blossomed from that unlikely beginning, and a close relationship had developed with the leader of their group, a husky witchdoctor whom we named Miguel.

Our contact with Miguel's people had been sporadic because of a vague animosity that existed between his village and the people on the big savannah, but once they realized we were alone, they began to appear with increasing regularity.

They apologized for having neglected us, and they explained that José had warned them against coming too often. The problem did not seem to be entirely because of the hard feelings between the two groups. Apparently, José had filed a claim on us! His discovery of Paul Dye and Dan Shaylor in the Shamatali village south of the big savannah had given him undisputed ownership of us all. We did our best to persuade them that we were public property, but although they humored us with agreeable smiles, they continued plans to curtail their visits as soon as José returned.

Miguel and his brother strode purposefully through the open door of our house one afternoon and came to a rigid halt in the center of the room. Their faces were smeared with red and purple dye, and they frowned as they clasped their bows and arrows stiffly to their chests.

Wally recognized their stance as the formal posture assumed by visiting men upon entering a village, and obliged by hurrying over with noisy exclamations of welcome. "Hah! Hah! You've arrived! My brothers have arrived! Hah!"

He waved his arms grandly, slapping his thighs as he chanted his glad-you-could-come phrases. The merriment in the eyes of the two visitors threatened to crumble the stern façade they struggled to present. The outsider's hilarious interpretation of a Yanoamö welcome was cramping their style.

Finally they could contain themselves no longer. They tried to suppress their smiles by clearing their throats, shifting position, and chanting; but it was hopeless. The formalities erupted in gales of laughter.

Miguel set his bow and arrows against the wall, and hugged Wally with both arms. "Brother! Wally!" he laughed, stomping his feet and whooping with joy. "You're doing great! You're really becoming one of us!"

Miguel's brother interrupted, shaking Wally by the arm. "Brother," he began, quivering with excitement, "next time you come to our village, do what we did just now! Don't just saunter in like a woman! Stand like a man, with your gun held against your chest, and we'll all holler a welcome! Let's make everybody laugh!"

The rest of Miguel's people who had arrived during the celebration had collected in the doorway, and when it seemed that our humble dwelling would not contain them all, we moved outside and settled around the campfire.

We were anxious to awaken their interest in spiritual things while we had the opportunity, but serious conversation was difficult. The women, especially, were too absorbed with our abnormalities to pay any heed to strange "fables" from the outside world. What ugly creatures we were!

They exclaimed over our hairy arms and pale skin, and fought for turns to run their hands over the stubble of Wally's day-old beard. Our legs were too long, our hair was too fine, and our eyes were too pale. Our insistence on remaining clothed was suspicious, and our faltering language ability gave rise to serious doubts about our humanity. Time had erased the initial curiosity of those who had constant contact with us, but for Miguel's people we were still exotic creatures to be examined in detail.

As they prepared to leave that afternoon, they told us they would be away for a few days. Rumor had it that raiders were once more prowling the nearby jungles, and the people thought it best to keep out of sight. Miguel's people had not become directly involved in the warfare, but their sympathy was definitely with the people on the big savannah, and they realized that a frustrated war party from the enemy village might well consider them to be worthy

The Big Savannah

alternatives. We were warned to keep away from the stream and to avoid leaving our homes during the night.

We had been by ourselves for a couple of days when a lone figure came over the hill and descended toward the airstrip. We congregated in front of the Hadleys' house to await our visitor, and were greeted by a young extrovert we later named Jaime. He already knew our names. He told us that he was from the Balafili valley, near the enemy village, and that his brother had been part of the crowd that had welcomed Derek to the big savannah a few weeks earlier.

Two young girls trailed behind him, and Jaime introduced them as his wives. They made a wide detour around us, and our new friend laughingly explained that they were afraid of Derek and Wally. They dashed past the house on the verge of tears and disappeared toward a tangle of shrubbery at the edge of the jungle where they were to set up their temporary shelter. Jaime taunted them for their fear and grinned a prediction that we would never see them again.

Jill and I accepted it as a challenge, and determined to win them over. We decided to tempt our timid guests with an invitation to a party. We prepared for an evening picnic around the campfire, complete with fresh bread, baked beans, roasted plantains and cinnamon rolls. Jaime, who was delighted with the idea, pointed out the trail the girls had taken and commissioned me to deliver the announcement when the meal was ready.

I started down the path, pausing and shouting every few moments, but no answer came. Jaime laughed uproariously and hollered in the same direction, adding that we wanted to feed them. Results were much better that time. The older girl came shyly to the edge of the bushes and held out her hand. But with every step I took forward, she retreated an equal distance.

Eventually I stood still and explained my mission. She declined the invitation but at the insistence of her husband finally agreed to come if she could bring her own food. She was not taking any chances. The younger one, who was hardly more than a child bride,

Treasures of Darkness

did not want to come under *any* condition.

Jaime demanded cooperation, and she burst into tears. I held my hand out toward her, promising protection from Wally and Derek, and her sobs subsided to an occasional shudder. I assured her that they would not sit near her, feed her, touch her, laugh at her, or look toward her. Hoping desperately in my reliability, she finally grabbed her mangy little dog and followed along behind us.

The two girls sat nervously on a log beside the fire, keeping a watchful eye on every movement Wally or Derek made. The girls tried to refuse the food we offered, but they occasionally yielded to our insistence only to pass it on to Jaime. Jill tried to tempt them with the frosting from a cinnamon roll. But they fed it to their dog. It did not really seem like a very successful venture.

Then for some unknown reason, the girls suddenly jumped to their feet, grabbed their baskets and dashed down the trail as fast as they could go. We looked at Jaime for a word of explanation, but he just shrugged and laughed. He reached for their bowls to clean up the leftovers and suggested that we might be able to win their confidence by inviting them to another party the following day.

Two days later they decided to return to their own village. Before they left, Jaime told us he wanted to bring some of his relatives over. He had seen our supply of trade goods, and he knew that his brothers and cousins would be eager to work for knives or machetes. To us, his offer was an opportunity to extend the potential influence of the Gospel to the Balafili valley, and we encouraged him to do so. Any willing workers would be a boon to the building program, and we would be able to establish new friendships at the same time.

We were still awaiting Jaime's return when the people of the big savannah came back from their jungle exile to the deserted village beside us. We saw them on the far side of the grassland, and we could not have been more excited had we heard the motor of an airplane! They stretched out in a long line as they made their way toward us, and I could hardly wait for the rowdy greeting that would mark an end to our solitude.

The Big Savannah

They hurried up the winding path that led to our doorstep, and swarmed around us enthusiastically, shouting and laughing their excitement. Had we missed them? Had we been frightened to stay alone? Did we still like them? Were we feeling generous? Had we seen any raiders? But there were some who seemed almost surprised to find us there, and their exclamations stirred uneasy feelings inside me. I wondered once more, for a fleeting moment, whether something really *had* been planned against us. Then I dismissed it from my mind as overly dramatic. No one deserved to be left to the mercy of an imagination like mine.

It was just as well that we were ignorant of the things that had been discussed in the village before they had left.

The enthusiasm of their return did not last long. They were soon chafing once more under the pressure of a potential enemy attack, and they took out their frustrations on one another and on us. The fact that visitors from Miguel's village and the Balafili valley had taken advantage of their absence to spend time with us did not help. They resented the fact that we had extended visiting and trading privileges to other people. Nor did it ease the situation when Jaime returned with his friends, resplendent in their finest beads and feathers, to meet the friendly outsiders who had won widespread fame as party givers.

The people who were sitting in our house at the time of Jaime's arrival got to their feet indignantly and left in a huff, and word soon spread through the village that we were entertaining strangers again.

The Balafili people Jaime had brought to meet us did not stay long. Once they realized that the people of the big savannah had returned to their village, they cut their visit short. But the damage was already done. As far as the people of the big savannah were concerned, our unfaithfulness had been proved beyond a shadow of a doubt.

The jealousy of some drove them to test our loyalty by making impossible demands for time and attention, and it resulted in bitter accusations that we always had time for other people, but not for them. Others repaid our infidelity by stealing everything they could lay their hands on, and by shouting insults. José delighted in tormenting Jill Hadley and me with obnoxious suggestions, and Timoteo seemed more belligerent than ever in his threats against Derek and Wally. The struggle to keep calm was exhausting, and we wore ourselves to a frazzle on the defensive end of every conversation.

The romance was gone, and I was completely deflated. The novelty of making new friendships was over. We were expending all our energies in a futile struggle to maintain a relationship that suddenly seemed hopelessly superficial. The entire proposition of introducing the gospel of Jesus Christ into the bedlam of the big savannah seemed an utter impossibility.

3

Marching as to War

Be strong in the grace that is in Christ Jesus.

2 Timothy 2:1

I grabbed a broom and scurried around the house in a cloud of dust, trying to take care of the morning chores before any visitors arrived from the village.

"Too late! Here come the women!" Wally laughed, stepping outside. "Sweep faster!"

The door banged behind him and he headed for Hadley's house. I could hear the happy shouts of greeting as he met the early morning visitors on the trail. "Wally! Brother! Where's Margarita? Is my dear old sister home?"

"She's downriver catching crabs!" Wally hollered over his shoulder. They hooted their reply and ran on toward us, laughing delightedly at the way he was catching on to the ridiculous answers that comprised so many Yanoamö jokes.

I watched the scramble as the women raced toward the house, squealing and laughing, with babies and baskets bouncing on their backs. It startled me to realize how eagerly I anticipated their visit. What a relief from the way I had been steeling myself against their incessant aggressiveness a few weeks earlier! I whispered my thanks to the Lord for prodding us into a new course of action.

We had taken a long, critical look at the situation that was driving us to distraction and decided the time had come to revise our strategy. Supposing that the constant complaints and demands of idle visitors had often resulted from boredom, we had begun to use the time they spent with us to better advantage. We decided to pursue *our* objectives as aggressively as they had been pursuing *theirs*, using each visit as an opportunity for teaching songs, testing our translation of Bible stories, introducing literacy, explaining Scripture, and otherwise increasing their field of knowledge in any way we could. And if our guests were adamantly uninterested in learning from us, we were prepared to learn from them. Armed with long lists of questions regarding their family relationships, language, history, and beliefs, we launched into a new offensive.

The daily routine suffered even more interruptions as we tried to put our new plan into effect, but it was well worth the effort. Both the Yanoamö and we were decidedly happier.

Enrique's mother burst through the door panting and giggling like a teenager, in spite of the fact that she was already the great grandmother of two children.

"Old woman!" I exclaimed, stretching my arms out to her. "You ran up the trail like a little girl!" She flung her arms around my waist, and while we exchanged hugs, the rest trooped in laughing exhaustedly and dropped their baskets to the floor.

"Little One," the old woman smiled, still breathing hard as she tugged me toward the bench, "come sit down." She pointed with her chin to a notebook that hung on a nail by the door. "Get it down," she laughed. "Let's listen to the paper!"

They scrambled for the prestigious seats beside me as I joined them on the bench. They were fascinated with the consistency of a written message, and never tired of testing the paper's memory by asking that I read notations they had dictated to me a few days earlier. The book was full of scribbled accounts of places they had been, animals they had seen, and food they had eaten, and it never failed to amaze them that the wording did not change no matter how much time had elapsed or who it was that read it.

Their enthusiasm had sprung from a pre-literacy campaign we had set in motion to stimulate interest in the wonders of the printed page. We had taken every possible opportunity to demonstrate its usefulness. They had been startled to realize that our books were able to remind us of words and phrases we had forgotten, and in an effort to explain the mechanics of it, we had invited them to dictate messages of their own and hear us read them back.

The idea that had gained the most popularity was that of recording their daily excursions to the jungles. That was what the women now had in mind. Many had begun coming to sign out as they left the village, and would return later on to see if the paper still remembered where they had been. It had become an intriguing pastime with a wide range of possibilities. Once in a while, exasperated mothers would arrive asking that we listen to the paper to find out where their sons had gone!

Voices of men coming up the trail drifted through the cracks in the wall, and a little girl was sent out to see who was approaching. She rushed back into the house whispering excitedly that Wally was coming with some men of a different family group, and the women hastily decided to abort their visit.

They had scarcely fled in a flurry of baskets and giggles when the men walked in.

Wally dragged a box of trade goods to the center of the floor, and the men huddled around it in sober appraisal of its contents. I backed away to the table to give them a little more room, and a little boy followed me, dancing happily up and down.

"What's my name?" he grinned, eyes sparkling with excitement. I studied his face for a long moment. Spanish names were getting to be a status symbol, especially among the younger set. They were delighted to be known by foreign words that were void of all the embarrassing and insulting connotations that usually accompanied their tribal names. Their age put them at a definite disadvantage, and the adults used their tribal names with a freedom that caused them considerable uneasiness.

"I don't think we named you yet," I answered.

He thrust a crumpled scrap of paper into my hand, and watched me smooth it out and read a note from Jill. *"We named this boy 'Tomasito,' but my marking pen is dry."*

"You're Tomasito, are you?" I exclaimed, reaching for a felt marker. He raised his eyebrows in silent affirmation and grinned shyly as he hopped closer and tapped himself on the chest. A moment later he was decorated with bold, red letters that proclaimed his new name. He climbed onto the bench with careful nonchalance, and waited for someone to notice.

None of his friends would be able to read it, but at least they would realize that his claims to a new name were valid. If they wanted to find out what it was, they could lead him to one of the outsiders for an interpretation of the wiggly lines that adorned him. In fact, the novel method of identification was more for our benefit than theirs. They often returned complaining that they had forgotten what we had named them, and many times we could not remember either!

The men who were congregated around the box of trade goods stretched to their feet and nodded solemnly as Wally reviewed the stipulations of a new work contract. They crowded close as he pulled a notebook from his pocket and began recording the details. In times past, he often had hired five men to work and been faced with ten expecting payment. Other times he had bargained for ten poles to be used in the building program and had been presented with eight. Now that our neighbors were catching on to the changeless quality of a written message, he had begun committing the details of such transactions to the infallible memory of the paper.

"What's your name?" he asked the first man.

"David," he answered gravely.

"And what are you asking for? Money?" David nodded, and Wally went on to record the number of poles David agreed to bring. Then he turned to a strong young man we knew only as Scar Shoulder.

"What's your name?" he queried, tongue in cheek. Scar Shoulder turned to the others around him.

"What shall I say?" he chuckled nervously. "He wants to know my name." They suggested he identify himself by his wife's name, since women's rights were not all that important, so he leaned forward, paused, and cleared his throat.

Marching as to War

"You can call me 'Bishajenami's Husband,'" he said. A quick grin flashed over Tomasito's face. He was not very practiced at deceit yet.

"I don't think he told you the truth," I murmured in English. Wally did not think so either, but he continued writing the details of each man's agreement. Then he motioned for silence, and assembled his workers to hear the final draft.

"It says that when David has brought me ten poles, I'll give him twelve large coins," he began, pausing for David's nod of approval. He studied the paper again and turned to Scar Shoulder. "When you've brought me ten poles," he began, "I'm going to give a large cooking pot to Bishajenami's Husband."

There was a startled silence before everyone burst into laughter with the realization that Scar Shoulder's trick was going to present a problem.

"No–no!" Scar Shoulder laughed, quickly stepping forward to correct the mistake. "Give it to *me!*" He whispered his own wife's name into Wally's ear, watched it duly recorded, and left with the others still laughing over the paper's strict regard for detail.

They returned a few days later, and scattered a group of boys who had been sitting in the doorway traveling to other continents via a battered, old "Viewmaster". The poles were counted, the paper was consulted, and each man's efforts were justly rewarded. Scar Shoulder reluctantly accepted the cooking pot he had requested. He studied it with mixed emotions. "Shall I take it?" he asked his cousin. "I'd really prefer an ax."

"No ax," Wally interrupted, reaching for his notebook. "It says right here–"

"Let *me* see that," Scar Shoulder laughed, snatching the book with sudden inspiration. "Let *me* hear what it says." He studied the writing with deep concentration. "It says I should have an ax," he pronounced, reluctantly retuning the book so Wally could check on his debt to David. "I heard it clearly."

The men crowded around Wally, solemnly studying the coins he dropped into David's hands one by one. We had taken advantage of the new interest in learning by introducing the Venezuelan currency and numbering system, but acceptance had been cautious. They could see no real value in the little pieces of metal that David had been collecting in a jar.

"Brother," David asked, "do I have enough yet? Can I get a hammock?"

Wally turned to the back of his notebook where he had kept a record of the money we were putting into circulation. Unless David had lost some, he should have had more than enough.

"I think so," Wally answered. "Send one of the boys to get your money jar." David looked blankly into Wally's face, as though he could not comprehend what he had heard. Gradually he allowed himself the thrill of expectancy, and his face broke into a wide smile.

"Really?" he grinned. "Right now?"

A child was quickly dispatched to the village, and the men settled down on the floor to await the moment of truth. For David's sake they hoped this experiment was going to be successful.

It was a big day for us, too. The system of bartering for the necessities of life had been loaded with pitfalls. Our neighbors had felt free to ask for anything they saw, supposing we would not display anything we were reluctant to give. One of two things always happened: either we flatly refused to consider parting with it, which was maddening to them, or we said it was available in exchange for something of equal value, which spoiled the fun entirely.

They were not interested in anything so businesslike. They sought a friendly trade relationship where they could freely ask of us, and we could freely ask of them, but such an arrangement had not seemed very practical to us. Before long, all our earthly goods would have been carted off to the village, and our house would have been heaped with baskets, gourds, and arrows, for which things we had little use.

We had attempted to reach an agreeable solution by offering to trade for food or labor. They did not find either idea particularly appealing, but were willing to give it a try. Our box of trade goods was soon depleted in exchange for mountains of bananas and plantains. We gave scissors for bananas, thread for bananas, and matches and fishhooks for bananas. We ate them ripe, we ate them green, we tried them boiled, fried, roasted, baked, and stewed. But the real problem came whenever someone tried to trade bananas for an ax or a machete. It would have taken four or five stalks of bananas to equal the price of one such item, and neither our houses nor our stomachs could stand the strain.

They had no concept of the value of labor, nor experience in the type of work we required. They had never built a square house, used a shovel, or leveled ground. They had a limited numbering system that met their needs, but they had been satisfied to think in vague generalities, and a request for ten hardwood poles was interpreted as "ten, more or less." Usually less. Our need for poles to be used in the superstructure of a permanent house presented the highest paying job, but it also involved the highest risk. Not many were willing to hazard a job that took them into the jungles.

We had introduced Venezuelan currency in two denominations they promptly tagged "mother coins" and "baby coins," and we encouraged their acceptance in exchange for food or labor. We promised to redeem them with trade goods whenever they presented us with a quantity of coins sufficient to equal the value of the item they wanted.

The first man who succumbed to our suggestion threw his money into the swamp on his way home, thoroughly disgusted with his own gullibility. Then David had accepted the challenge and begun collecting coins in an empty jar provided for that purpose. Now the day of reckoning had come.

Before long, a horde of David's friends and relatives arrived and grimly presented him with his jar of money. They gathered around him protectively, silently defying us to tell him, as we had often done before, that he did not have enough yet.

The house was quiet and still, in spite of the large crowd that had collected. David soberly handed his bank to Wally. He dumped the contents into his hand and began dropping them back into the jar, one by one. "*Uno, dos, tres–*" Wally began, taking advantage of the situation for a short lesson in Spanish.

No one spoke a word as Wally finished counting. Then David searched his face for a hint of satisfaction.

"What did he say?" someone whispered as Wally turned and disappeared into the back room.

"He didn't say anything," David answered nervously. Beads of perspiration stood out on his forehead, but he grinned confidently when he noticed that I was watching him.

Then Wally swept into the room wrapped elegantly in a red and yellow hammock. The shouts and laughter that filled the house threatened to lift the roof! David struggled to maintain a calm exterior, but when Wally insisted on dancing a jig to show off the brilliance of the new hammock, he could scarcely contain himself.

There was a mad scramble as all of David's relatives grabbed for the prize. Scar Shoulder held one end, David's brother took the other, and David climbed aboard. He spread out luxuriously and grinned at his family staring in awe. The new hammock that was finally his had little resemblance to the crude bark hammocks that hung in the roundhouse, and he smiled gracious acceptance of their admiration.

From that time on, everyone clamored for empty bottles. The magic of money was discussed far and wide, and I overheard one of David's relatives explaining the intricacies of big-time finance to a less informed friend. "You just have to collect little pieces of metal in a jar," he said enthusiastically, "and when it's full, you get whatever you want–free!"

The enthusiasm for learning was reflected in the spiritual realm as well. We seized every opportunity for teaching stories that would lay a groundwork on which to build the gospel–creation, the fall of man, Noah, and Elijah. Similar legends of their own lent the Bible stories a credibility that could not be ignored, and once they realized the source of our information, they never questioned the validity of our accounts. Ours had been permanently recorded on paper, and no one would dispute the reliability of a written message.

They struggled to understand.

Marching as to War

Enrique continued to listen with quiet thoughtfulness. Was it really possible to be cleansed from sin? Could guilt really be taken away? Julio, José's brother, spent long hours with Derek, irresistibly drawn by the message that offered eternal life. It sounded too good to be true. Was there really more than a lonely, wandering spirit-life on the other side of death?

God's love seemed easy to understand. They could not see any reason why He *would not* love them. But His hatred for sin was puzzling. Neither the indifferent creator of their own legends nor the tempermental spirits who indwelt their witchdoctors had ever concerned themselves with matters of conscience, and they had never realized that such things mattered to anyone. They did not find the possibility particularly reassuring. Stories of God's judgment made them defensive and uneasy. Death was a possibility they refused to consider.

Then a calamity in José's household brought eternity very close.

Julio died. His death came suddenly, following an undiagnosed sickness that lasted only three days, and he was promptly avenged by his brothers. They attributed his fatal illness to witchcraft and retaliated in kind. On a secret mission to a faraway Shamatali village, they evened the score by blowing a powdered curse on the path that led from the village they held responsible.

Laughing Lady stopped laughing. She was Julio's stepmother, and the two had enjoyed a close relationship. I never mentioned his death to her, because I had been away when it occurred, getting our two oldest children settled in school. Now that it was already history, tribal taboos strongly discouraged any mention of the subject.

She came for a visit after I returned, complaining that she was getting thin. "Don't you have any food?" I asked as she settled down beside me on a log by the campfire.

"Yes," she shrugged. "But I don't feel like eating."

She kept her eyes on the ground. Her face was streaked with the black smudges of mourning. "You're too sad to eat," I sympathized, hinting at the real problem and wondering how far I could go without offending her.

Treasures of Darkness

She looked up, crying a little, and shifted closer toward me. "You weren't here," she whispered fiercely. "We were all angry while you were away."

"Wally told me about it," I whispered, nodding.

"Little One," she said, hesitating a moment, "where is he?" I was silent, and she asked more pointedly, "Is he with God?"

"I don't know," I answered. "God says He will save anyone who trusts Him, and God doesn't lie. He wouldn't deceive anyone."

"Did he trust Him?" she persisted. She searched my eyes so earnestly, pleading for an answer that would give consolation. But what could I say? I turned my eyes away.

"I don't know. Derek often talked with him. He told him to put his trust in God, but I don't really know whether he did."

"Of *course* he didn't!" she hissed. "How can we believe what you say when we don't understand what you mean?" Her face was filled with utter despair, and she spoke the most potent, challenging words I had ever heard. "None of us know what it's really about. We *want* God, but we don't *know* Him. You've got to help us! You've got to teach us quickly! Whatever will become of us?"

I was chasing chickens out of the house a few days later when Laughing Lady returned with a group of women. We had finally moved from Paul and Dan's little shack into our permanent home. It was only a glorified mud hut with an aluminum roof, and it still lacked an outside wall on one side. She called to me through the window and invited me to sit outside with them for a while. They wanted to learn a new song and listen to the paper.

We talked for a while, practiced a Yanoamö version of "Do Lord" that the songwriter would never have recognized, and spent a few moments discussing eternal life.

The questions they asked reflected some serious thinking. What was heaven really like? Could people eat there? Are there plantains? Do the angels ever fight? Is God frightening? Does He know how to make hammocks, or would they have to take their own?

Laughing Lady shushed everyone with an impatient wave of her hand. She leaned forward to whisper something into my face, and

Marching as to War

the others crowded around to hear my answer. "Margarita," she began, "did you used to carry a basket on your back like we do?"

The intense expressions on the faces that breathlessly awaited my reply made me uneasy, though the question did not seem too complicated. I answered negatively, and they seemed disappointed.

"Oh. Didn't you *ever*?" I obligingly rephrased my answer and said that my ancestors had probably toted baskets long ago.

"But then you quit, didn't you?" Laughing Lady accused. "And you don't eat tadpoles, either!"

I realized I was playing right into their hands, but as I envisioned the slimy black masses of tadpoles they collected in the swamp, I could not help cheerfully confessing that she was right again.

She straightened up. Like a smug, confident lawyer she concluded her case against me. "And you always wear clothing," she said. "And you can't talk straight!"

At that point I asked what it was all about. She hesitated a moment, as if she were being called upon to say something that might be offensive. "We think that if we accept the gospel we might become like you."

There was a heavy silence. Everyone watched me anxiously, wondering if I would be angry. I struggled for sobriety.

"Our country is far, far away from here," I whispered, trying to inject a note of annoyance in my voice for the geographical barriers that had separated our cultures. "No wonder we've never been able to do the same things and speak the same language! Even the Shamatali people can't talk the way you do, and they live just a day's travel downriver!" There were murmurs of agreement. "But anyway," I smiled, "you don't have to be like us outsiders in order to become children of God."

Their expressions indicated surprise, so I pursued the matter further, explaining that God liked them as they were. I told them that His promises were not only for outsiders, that eating tadpoles was not wrong, and that God had never condemned the practice of carrying pack baskets. "Those things don't matter," I assured them. "It's your hearts God wants to change. Your hearts are sad and worried."

Silently they nodded their agreement. They made no sophisticated attempts at hiding their fears. They whispered angrily back and forth for a moment or two concerning the cruelty of spirits and the futility of death. Laughing Lady pulled a needle from her wooden earplug and began digging a sliver from her little boy's foot. "That's right," she whispered angrily. "That's the truth. We don't know *how* to be happy."

There were a few moments of reflective silence. As though startled by her own admission, she abruptly looked up from her work and laughed loudly. Giving her little boy a sharp slap for crying, and telling him he could *keep* his sliver, she stuck the needle back into her earplug and scrambled to her feet. The others took their cue from her and reached for their baskets. The meeting was over.

"Well, I surely wouldn't want to end up speaking like you!" Laughing Lady smiled in an attempt to direct the conversation away from the painful realities of life. She hitched her basket into a comfortable position. "Can we still catch crabs when we're Christians?"

She did not bother to wait for an answer. Giving her little boy a shove in the right direction, she headed down the path to the jungle. "We'll be back tomorrow," she called over her shoulder. "Don't be lonely while we're gone!"

We began holding regular meetings in the center of the village clearing and prepared a large chart depicting the broad way to destruction and the narrow way to life. Their interest was completely captivated, and word of the chart spread quickly to surrounding villages. Miguel's people hurried across the savannah to find out what it was all about, and a delegation from the Balafili valley arrived with a request that someone take the message to the people of their area, too.

We had classified the villages of the Balafili valley into three basic divisions. The most distant group was the one to which the people of the big savannah referred as their enemies. Friends of the enemy village made up the second group. Their settlement was two

Marching as to War

or three hours' walk closer to us, and their involvement in the warfare was limited to the moral support they offered their neighbors. A neutral village near them made up the final category and provided the link we needed with the Balafili population. It was from that village that Jaime had first come with his two timid wives; it was from that village that visitors had since come from time to time; and it was from that village that we now received a plea for teaching.

One day the porch door slammed, and we turned to see an elaborately decorated visitor standing stiffly in the center of the room with his bow and arrows clasped to his chest. He was a sturdily built man in his late thirties, and Wally grinned as he recognized the self-styled Balafili leader behind the purple dye and blue feathers. It was Samuel, a man of staggering self-confidence who neither felt intimidated by the outside world nor obliged to assert his independence of it.

He was a close friend and relative of Enrique and had made several trips to the big savannah for the express purpose of hearing the message we taught. He had been a witchdoctor of wide renown, but from the day he first heard the Gospel, he had pursued a knowledge of the Lord with singleness of heart. His sporadic contact with us had made it difficult to determine the extent of his spiritual insight, but there was no doubting the fact that Samuel fully believed all he understood.

We hurried to the porch and greeted him with all the hullabaloo due his position, and by the time the formalities were over, the rest of his party had filed in.

Before they left, Samuel managed to extract a promise from Derek and Wally that they would plan a monthly tour of the villages in his area to explain the message of the two ways. He calmly informed us that he had already taught his people everything he knew, and he apologized for the fact that he could not answer all the questions his teaching was engendering.

Wally volunteered to make the first trip, and a guide was sent from Samuel's village to conduct him on the eight-hour hike over the mountains.

Treasures of Darkness

It was still daylight when they arrived, and after allowing Wally a short rest, Samuel gathered his people together to hear the message of the chart.

They squatted in the village clearing in typical disarray–women talking, children playing, scrawny dogs running through the crowd. The men shuffled as close as possible to Wally, and Samuel helped explain each picture as they struggled to focus their eyes on the strange drawings before them.

Then Wally took over and drew their attention to the rough cross that stood at the entrance of the narrow way. It was a picture of two poles lashed together, and Wally explained that Jesus was killed on a similar cross. He died in our place, and faith in His name provides access to the way of eternal life.

Samuel studied the crowd uneasily. He knew they had trouble comprehending the message. He stood up to take the floor again. "God says our innermost beings are unclean because of our sin, but the blood of His Son makes us acceptable."

The congregation broke into loud debate. "But *I'm* not unclean," one of them protested. "What have you ever seen *me* doing?"

"No–don't say that," Samuel corrected him, pointing to the crowd on the broad way. "Is it just adultery that leads us to destruction? No! Some of these people are just gossiping. Some are stealing. Some are fighting."

They looked a little dismayed. If all those things fell into the same category, what hope was there for anyone?

"But the paper says that when you admit your guilt, He doesn't get angry," Samuel hastened to assure them. "He cleanses you. Only those who deny having done anything wrong continue to travel the broad way."

They returned to their hammocks as darkness fell, but not for long. Their curiosity regarding the message had been temporarily satisfied, but their inquisitiveness concerning the messenger had only begun. One by one they drifted to Samuel's shelter and formed a tight crowd around Wally's hammock. They brought green plantains with them, and roasted their bedtime snacks on Wally's campfire while they prodded him for the details of our courtship and marriage.

"Brother, did you feed Margarita from the time she was a baby, or did you yank her away from her mother when she was full grown?"

"Neither," Wally replied. "I didn't *have* to yank her. She came willingly!"

"Ah Wally! Ah Margarita!" they screamed with delight. "Did she really fall in love with you?" They shook with laughter and crowded closer to listen to his embarrassing confessions. Such a dull wedding was strictly second-rate. Did none of her relatives offer any resistance at all? They must have been glad to get rid of her!

"Wally," Samuel said, in an attempt to rescue his friend's masculinity, "she may have been willing—but you yanked her from her mother anyhow. Isn't that right?"

Wally had to confess that it was not.

"But you *did* pay for her?" he suggested? "You *did* take meat to her father, didn't you?"

A confused whispering interrupted the question while the others nudged Samuel and told him not to ask questions that might make Wally angry. "It's all right," Samuel whispered. "He's already told me about his father-in-law. He's alive. You can talk about him." So the interrogations wandered away from the subject of our marriage, and turned to investigations of our family history.

One by one they finally disappeared to the comfort of their hammocks. Still in a jovial mood, they began hollering through the darkness to one another. Jaime called out to Samuel, "Did you see me hunting today?"

"Where did you go?" Samuel chuckled, entering into Jaime's game.

"Downstream by the big cashew tree. Have you found me?"

"Yes! I've found you! You mean past the cashew tree and beside the little thorn bush near the stream. Have you found me?"

"I see you! You mean the rock that's upstream from the anthill! Have you found me?"

On and on the game went, with voices laughing out suggestions as the word game progressed. But sleep finally overtook them, fires

Treasures of Darkness

flickered out, and conversation faded to restful silence.

Long before the first rays of morning light pierced the darkness of the village, Samuel awakened and swung gently in his hammock, chanting a greeting to the new day. For twenty minutes or so, his low, mournful monotone was the only sound in the stillness. Then one by one the campfires were blown to flame, and family groups became silhouetted around their hearths.

The sun was still low in the morning sky when Wally and Samuel set out for a tour of the surrounding villages. They were warmly received by each group, and the interest that was shown testified to Samuel's concern for his neighbors. Everyone had heard of the promise of eternal life, and all were eager to learn more.

But Samuel was not above using the new message as a weapon when the occasion so permitted. At one village they encountered a group of people who enthusiastically hoped for the destruction of everyone on the big savannah, and Samuel wasted no time denouncing the warfare that had erupted between his friends and theirs. Before Wally even had a chance to explain his mission, Samuel had unfurled the chart and begun an explanation of the two ways.

"People who creep in ambush, waiting to shoot their neighbors, are right here on this wide road," he said, directing their attention to the figures on the chart. "See where the trail ends? They all fall into hell."

Their tour of villages took them up and down the grassy slopes of the Balafili valley, and Samuel paused on the top of a hill to point out the general locality of other nearby populations. "Far over that way," he said, "is the village that sends raiders to the big savannah."

"Will you take me there?" Wally asked.

Samuel's face froze in stony silence. He jerked his head angrily before he answered. "No," he said. "They'd kill me."

"Some other day?" Wally suggested. "Sometime when the fighting is over?"

"It will never be over," Samuel stated flatly. "Not until they've

Marching as to War

completely wiped each other out. I'm weary of trying to stop them. I'm through interfering." His tone did not encourage further discussion of the subject, but Wally knew him well enough to realize that the matter was not beyond consideration. There had to be a way of negotiating peace between the two villages, and Samuel was a natural diplomat.

After a well-earned rest back on the big savannah, Wally joined Derek for an afternoon visit to the village. Everyone asked for news of their enemies. Had Wally seen them? Had he heard any rumors? Were the plantains in the Balafili gardens ready to be harvested? As long as the plantains were small, the people on the big savannah could relax. Their enemies would not send a raiding party without first holding a memorial feast in honor of the dead they wanted to avenge, and no feast could be prepared until the gardens allowed it.

Wally and Derek wandered around the circle of the village, stopping here and there to share some verses from 2 Peter. The Scripture portions that had been translated into the lowland dialect had not been very useful in the highlands, and they wanted to test the effectiveness of some revisions. Scar Shoulder called out to them as they passed by and invited them to read to his family.

They were offered firewood on which to sit, and Scar Shoulder squatted on the floor beside them, calling for silence. He listened with amused tolerance as they explained how both Yanoamö and outsider alike had forsaken the right way and gone astray. He smiled his understanding as they told of the sacrifice God had made in order to reconcile men to Himself.

"Come back again," he grinned, getting to his feet as Wally and Derek prepared to move on. "Come back tomorrow and teach me those words again." But none of them could know that tomorrow would be too late.

4

The Battle Begins

The dark places of the earth are full of the habitations of cruelty.

Psalm 74:20

We were still sleeping when Scar Shoulder and a group of relatives stopped by the house in the darkness of the predawn. "Brother! Wally!" a feminine voice shouted. "I'm not working today! Don't wait for me!" It sounded like Scar Shoulder's cousin, a woman who had been helping mix adobe for the walls of the porch. "Wally! Wake up!" she yelled insistently. "I said I'm going downriver with my cousins! We'll be back later!"

Wally grunted a sleepy response, and the party moved on.

With breakfast over, Wally was poring over a few verses from 2 Peter when a frenzied commotion in front of the house caught our attention. We raced to the front door in time to see a man who had been sharpening his machete jump to his feet in a fierce, uncontrollable rage. His eyes were wild, and his mind seemed paralyzed by a sudden, consuming fury. He screamed like an animal and groped blindly for the bow and arrows he had left by our front door. Grasping them tightly in his hand, he tore down the path to the roundhouse, shouting a raider alarm.

A young boy who had apparently brought the news followed behind him, weeping bitterly. A cold fear gripped me, and my heart pounded in my throat. This was no false alarm.

The crowd that gathered in front of our house silently watched the grim warriors race down the path. We stood with the Hadleys

The Battle Begins

in the crowd, waiting nervously for a verified report and trying to convince ourselves that it probably was not true.

A young mother ran down the trail with her baby slung at her side. "My brother!" she wailed. "Oh, my brother!" We knew she did not have any brothers, and we could not decide to whom she was referring. I moved to her side and whispered to her.

"Who is it? Who do you call your brother?"

A second woman grabbed me roughly by the arm and pulled me away. "Don't ask her like that! Don't say that!" she hissed angrily. "It was the one who went downriver to hunt early this morning."

She could see that we still did not know who had been shot. "It was Isabela," she whispered. The young mother beside us burst into fresh sobs at the mention of Scar Shoulder's wife. Jill and I looked at each other with bewilderment. Were the raiders really angry enough to shoot women? Someone crowded in beside us, and I asked incredulously if Isabela had really been killed.

"Oh!" she exclaimed in disgust. "It was the *man!*"

"The *man?*" I gasped, stunned by the possibility that Scar Shoulder could suddenly be dead. "Isabela's husband?"

"Hah! Be quiet!" she screamed, as I made another reference to him. The death taboos were already in effect. Obviously, we were supposed to draw our own conclusions.

There was a respectful silence as Isabela approached us, crying brokenheartedly. She had not gone with the others that morning, and had just heard the news in the village. Her steps were mechanical, and she seemed in a state of shock as she passed by with her baby hugged to her bosom. Oblivious to the sympathetic eyes that followed her, she disappeared down the trail the hunting party had taken earlier.

"Which way will they bring him back?" I asked one of the women.

"Right here. Right past your house," she answered. "But they won't be back for a long time. He's heavy."

She looked at me with eyes that warned against asking any more. No one knew his condition, and there was nothing to do but wait and see.

Treasures of Darkness

An hour or so later, a slow procession emerged from the jungle and wound its way across the savannah. They were not using the path that led directly to our houses. My stomach tightened in a hard knot with the realization that he was not considered a candidate for medical aid.

We moved hesitantly toward the runway as they approached. We wanted to be nearby if they needed help, and respectfully distant in case it was too late.

Scar Shoulder's father carried him on his back. The anguish on his face as he turned toward us stung our eyes with tears. He halted and opened his mouth as if to speak, then thought better of it. Shifting the weight of his heavy burden, he silently turned and continued on his way to the village.

Tribal taboos forbade our asking the questions we wondered, so Wally followed them, gradually catching up with the old man so he could satisfy himself that there was nothing we could do. Scar Shoulder's legs had been bent at the knee, and his feet tied up with a vine to keep them from dragging. His head bounced limply against his father's at every step. A deep, wide hole in his side showed where an arrow had sunk into his body, and he was covered with blood.

We stood by the edge of the airstrip long after the mournful group passed by, and we listened with mute sorrow to the death wail that rose from the village. The long-awaited raiders had finally struck, and cheerful, amiable Scar Shoulder had entered violently into eternity.

The day dragged on. I kept finding myself in a dream, reflecting on the past and searching my memory for any clue that might have suggested Scar Shoulder had believed the gospel. But there was none. My mind drifted back to our first encounter, nine months earlier, when we had first become aware of him as an individual among the sea of faces that surrounded us.

I remembered him squatting on the floor listening soberly as Wally told of the judgment God was going to bring on the world because of sin. "Do you know God?" he had asked Wally, and upon hearing an affirmative reply, had demanded that we use our

The Battle Begins

influence to persuade Him not to do it. The power of a witchdoctor had always been judged by his dominance of the spirits, and it had puzzled him to realize that Wally was willingly subordinate to the Lord. He had nodded his head as Wally had encouraged him to take advantage of the salvation God offered, but his interest had not lasted long.

Time passed, and no fire and brimstone fell from the sky. Scar Shoulder felt no urgency. "I'm not going to die!" he would laugh. "I'm not old or sick, and I'm too cautious to be shot!" But his minutes were ticking away faster than any of us realized.

He had brought his wife, Isabela, for a visit a month or so earlier. Talking across the partition that divided the porch from the kitchen, we had enjoyed a good time together discussing their first baby, who was soon to arrive. "It's going to be a boy," Isabela had confided, whispering with giddy excitement. "We're going to have lots of boys!" Like most of the men, her husband had been embarrassed by such sentiment, but had smiled grudgingly as Isabela and I had made plans for the new baby.

Then one afternoon I had recognized his voice calling me to the porch. I was busy in another room, and had not responded immediately. He kept calling and finally added, "The one you've been waiting to see is here!" It took a few seconds before I realized the baby must have arrived. They were all smiles as I hurried toward them. Isabela grinned widely through layers of dirt and grime, and held up her little son for inspection. She hadn't bathed since her baby's birth three days earlier, and a dirtier pair would have been difficult to imagine. I pretended he was clean and sweet-smelling, imagined a diaper on him, and held out my arms. Isabela handed him to me, enjoying the praise I lavished on him. Scar Shoulder grinned with justifiable pride and struggled for nonchalance.

Now his little one was a week old and fatherless.

Scar Shoulder's body was dropped into a hammock in the center of the family's cramped living area. There it stayed for over a day and a half. Immobilized by shock, his father did not send the men to gather wood for a funeral pyre until late the following day.

Treasures of Darkness

A huge fire was built in front of the dead man's shelter. Then his body, hammock and all, was thrown into the flames and quickly covered with sticks of wood. By the time the hysterical screams subsided to a mournful wailing, Scar Shoulder had been reduced to a scattering of white bone among the smoldering embers.

Two weeks later, when the initial shock of Scar Shoulder's death was over, sorrow gave way to anger, and the attention of the village shifted toward a rapid reprisal. We began offering cautious suggestions for ending the warfare, and though they listened to our suppositions that the enemy village might be willing to consider a truce now that they had avenged at least one of their men, no one was willing to pay such a price for peace. They could not view their loss so objectively.

Scar Shoulder's grandfather organized a hunting party that was sent out to dig some armadillos from their burrows for a memorial feast. While the hunters were away, Scar Shoulder's mother went to the family garden with a group of women and destroyed the crops her son had planted. She wanted no reminders of her grief, and she did not intend to let anyone reap the benefits of her son's work now that he himself had been denied the pleasure of enjoying the fruit of his labors. They carried home baskets of plantains and hung them in their shelters to ripen for the feast.

The nights were filled with chanting and tears, and when the hunters returned, the proceedings got under way.

The ripened plantains were cooked to a watery sauce in a large, blackened cooking pot, and the meat was stacked beside it. Scar Shoulder's relatives had cried most of the day, and the din of their wailing grew wilder as a crowd collected around their shelter. An angry group of warriors, assuming stiff, formal stances like an honor guard at a funeral, clacked their bows and arrows together ominously, and shouted their fury against the enemy village.

The crying verged on hysteria. One of the men reached for a specially prepared gourd, and the warriors crowded around the mother's hearth as the memorial service came to a grisly climax. It was one of four gourds in which Scar Shoulder's crushed bones had been placed following his cremation. A little of the crushed bones

The Battle Begins

was mixed with some plantain sauce and handed to the mother. She drank it all to the accompaniment of loud, anguished screams, then burned the empty container in the flames of her campfire. The men grimly stirred their portions of the white powder into more sauce they scooped from the kettle, and drank to a successful retaliation.

José stood to his feet, grabbed his bow and arrows, and took up a ceremonial stance before the crowd. "All right," he chanted, with barely controlled emotion. "Who's standing with me? Who's going with me?" One by one, others joined him in a tight circle as they committed themselves to avenging Scar Shoulder's death.

Some declined for reasons of age or health, and the fearful were not expected to go.

Timoteo stood. He did not share José's reckless determination, but he was a good strategist, and his organizational abilities spread confidence. His nephews joined him. David stood. He was in turmoil. His conscience nagged him, but his sense of responsibility spurred him on. Enrique's brother stood, and all eyes turned toward Enrique, but he sat where he was.

He had neither asked our advice nor told us of the conflict in his heart, and we were completely unaware of the spiritual battle that was raging simultaneously with the physical. It was now or never. He steeled himself against the startled, angry expressions around him. Relative or not, he was through with warfare. His understanding of the Gospel may have been limited, but his choice was plain. He had decided on the narrow way to Life, and he was prepared to walk it alone.

The remaining food was distributed among the mourners, and each returned to his own shelter.

Early the next morning, José strode to the center of the village clearing and called for the warriors to join him in a formal display of strength before they left. One by one, they took their places beside him, clacking their arrows together impatiently. Then amid impassioned appeals to wipe them all out and be careful, a party of fifteen men filed grimly out of the village.

A flurry of excitement arose when they returned a few days later.

Treasures of Darkness

One woman ran quickly down the path to our house screaming for her children to get home immediately lest they be strangled by raiders. The mission had been a success. They had stirred the anger of the enemy village once more, and a new era of fear had begun. Another man had been killed and had to be avenged.

A few weeks later Samuel arrived with news from the Balafili valley. He sat in the porch with Wally and talked of inconsequential matters until he was asked if there were any reports from the enemy village. His face sobered and he looked at Wally blankly, as though he did not know how to begin. Then he blurted out his message. "They say they're going to kill you."

Samuel did not know how Wally would receive such news, and he searched his face for a reaction that might have warned him against continuing. "They say that because you have decided to defend these people with your shotgun, they're going to count *you* as an enemy, too."

"I never said that," Wally said, frowning over the strange report.

"Maybe not," Samuel shrugged. "But that's what they say."

They sat in silence for a few moments, puzzled over Wally's sudden involvement in the warfare. Wally saw no alternative but to go to the enemy village himself and convince them of his neutrality.

"Samuel," he said, "would you take me to talk with them?" Samuel jerked his head angrily. It was out of the question. "Are you afraid to go?" Wally persisted. "Would it be dangerous?"

Samuel nodded. The friendship he had once enjoyed with the enemy village had come to an automatic halt when he had continued visiting the people of the big savannah. He just could not go, and that was final.

Wally got up and walked to the window. Samuel followed him with his eyes. "Wally," he whispered, "be careful."

Wally did not answer right away, and when he did it was obvious that the Yanoamö were influencing him more than I had realized! Their maddening habit of responding to serious moments with frivolity must have been contagious. He stuck out his chest

The Battle Begins

and slapped his thighs in imitation of the way men often responded to such advice.

"Of *course* I'll be careful!" he mimicked, in a high, excited falsetto. "They won't shoot *me*!"

Samuel jumped to his feet and faced him, wiping a smile from his face with the back of his hand. He began to chant, swaying back and forth in front of Wally as he worked up steam for a full-fledged performance. "Brother–Wally–You're absolutely right! Absolutely right! They'll *never* shoot you! You're the bravest man I know! You're stealthy in the jungles! You're wary! Your aim is deadly!"

He gained momentum as he continued, and the chanting grew in intensity with every line. So did the sarcasm. "You're indestructible! You're so very strong! You always carry your own things on the trail and never need help with anything! You know your way all through the jungles, and you can find the trail to any village you care to visit!"

Samuel could not keep a straight face any longer. Wally had long since broken into a grin, and without his serious participation, Samuel could not concentrate on the rhythm of his chant. "Ah Wally!" he whooped, collapsing on a bench in convulsive laughter.

"Brother," he smiled, as he regained his composure, "be careful anyway."

"I will," Wally nodded. "I will."

A few weeks later, when we realized that an unscheduled flight was going to be made in order to fly a new missionary family to join us on the big savannah, Wally began making plans to visit the enemy village. He shared his idea with Paul Dye by radio, and Paul offered to accompany him.

They flew to a small landing strip near Samuel's village on the same flight that brought Paul and Marty Shadle to join us with their two small children. Arrangements were made for the plane to pick them up the following day when the last of the Shadles' supplies had been flown in from a lowland location.

Wally and Paul spent the first night in Samuel's shelter and shared an illustrated story of Lazarus and the rich man with an enthusiastic audience. Samuel borrowed the pictures when they were finished, rolled them into a scroll, and tucked them into his quiver. Everyone finally drifted off to his own hammock, and Wally and Paul sat around the fire to discuss their plans with Samuel.

He agreed to take them to the enemy village. It sounded daring, but if they were willing to risk it, so was he. The three of them left early the following day. As they neared enemy territory, Samuel grew anxious over the fact that he had armed himself only with a machete. He stopped the little party and warned that from then on they would have to be extra quiet and extra quick. They could not afford to be detected on the trail. They had to get right into the village clearing before their presence was discovered, lest their intentions be misinterpreted. Their connection with the big savannah made them highly suspect, and their visit could easily be construed as aggression.

All went well until they neared the village, when a woman returning with a load of firewood spied them on the trail and screamed a blood-curdling raider alarm to alert her people.

Samuel spun to face Wally and Paul. "Run!" he yelled. "RUN!"

For a split second Wally was not sure whether they were supposed to run toward the village or away from it, but when Samuel made a mad dash for the enemy roundhouse they followed closely behind him.

An old man had been walking near the village when the woman's alarm was sounded. Terror stricken, he ran for the safety of his home, but was overtaken by Samuel before he reached his destination. In sudden panic, Samuel seized the old man's bow and arrows and tried to wrestle them from his grip. He grappled desperately for the weapons as he ran on, dragging the old man behind him.

Time did not allow further struggle. Samuel gave up, tightened his grip on his machete, and sprinted for the entrance of the village, but he arrived a second too late. The opening was barricaded with poles.

The surprise entrance they had planned was now an impossibility, and the alternatives were not appealing. They could neither leave nor enter without facing the risk of being shot.

The Battle Begins

They halted a moment, a little undecided as to the best course of action. The old man who had denied Samuel his bow and arrows caught up with them there, and stepping carefully to one side motioned for Samuel to remove the poles that blocked the entrance to the village clearing.

Giving Wally and Paul tense instructions to stand back, Samuel dislodged the poles one by one. There was a deathly silence inside, and Samuel worked quickly and cautiously. He soon had removed enough poles to allow passage through the barricade. All that remained was to steel himself against the possibility of being shot as he stepped into the opening.

Motioning for Wally and Paul to follow him, he took a deep breath and stepped quickly into the enemy roundhouse.

The situation was too strained to allow a cool, objective view of the reaction as they strode briskly to the center of the clearing, but the customary pandemonium of greeting that finally broke the stillness was music to their ears.

An old man approached them, asking in a soft chant why the outsiders had come. Paul immediately recognized him. When he and Dan Shaylor had first arrived on the big savannah to clear a landing strip, they had done some vaccinating in the other villages of the Balafili valley and had met the same old man in a village where he had been visiting friends.

"Ah! My father!" Paul exclaimed. "Do you remember me? You're the one I called 'father' when we were giving injections to ward off the measles epidemic!"

The old man eyed him silently for a moment, and then responded in a slow smile, welcoming his son to the village. Everyone relaxed.

The original commotion died down, and the men began yelling hurried instructions to the women to prepare food for their guests. The outsiders rested in hammocks offered by their hosts, and the braver souls of the village gathered around to study them.

Samuel was causing quite a stir, too. It had been a long time since he had been there, and the accusations that had mounted against him during the months of warfare were all unleashed in a ceremonial chant.

Samuel and his accuser faced one another in the village clearing, and while they straightened out their problems in the approved Yanoamö style, Samuel remembered the pictures of Lazarus and the rich man he had rolled up and shoved inside his quiver. Without a pause in the chanting, he reached over his shoulder, grabbed his quiver, and pulled it around in front of him so he could take off the top and shake out its contents. He handed the scroll to a curious child standing nearby, and sent him with it to Paul and Wally.

The people gathered eagerly to see if the paper really had a message. They had long ago heard rumors concerning the magic of literacy, and they discussed each picture with animated enthusiasm. They nodded vigorous agreement as the Gospel was presented, though they probably did not comprehend its personal implications. Then Wally and Paul referred to the warfare with the people on the big savannah, and everyone lapsed into a silence so oppressively heavy that it seemed deafening.

Paul and Wally told them that we outsiders were neutral. We wanted to be friends with all of them. They nodded silently. Wally explained how he had tried to discourage our people from avenging Scar Shoulder's death. No answer. They just rocked on their haunches, elbows on their knees and hands clenched in front of their mouths. The subject was not open to discussion. They had no intention of dropping the fight.

The Missionary Aviation Fellowship pilot, Paul Johnson, was scheduled to land on the tiny strip near Samuel's village in a few more hours. Casting about for a good excuse for a return visit, Paul decided to buy some deer meat from one of the men—on credit. Trading was a sure sign of friendship; and when Paul offered to bring a knife the next time in exchange, the deal was accepted enthusiastically, and they were invited to return as soon as possible.

They gathered their things together and were soon hurrying back down the trail to Samuel's village.

The Battle Begins

Rainy season passed in a series of grueling hours of desk work, days of discouragement, refreshing intervals of spiritual interest, and hair-raising raider alarms. Not even Timoteo or José could match the fury Isabela would display on such occasions. Paul and Marty Shadle began serious language study; Jill and I wearied ourselves with revisions of literacy material; and Wally and Derek continued translating Bible stories.

We were encouraged by the individual responses of many, but no one was free to live unto himself. They may not all have agreed with the retaliation against the enemy village, but the resulting danger had to be shared equally. The village was often evacuated for a few days as they sought respite from fear of ambush.

Their jungle campouts were not without complications. Scattered as they were through the woods, even the minimal social restraints of communal life in the roundhouse were inoperable, and they battled a succession of fights and squabbles resulting from thievery, gossip, and immorality. They always returned with the complaint that they had forgotten everything we had ever taught them. It seemed that way to us, too. We would nod weary agreement and start over again, reminding ourselves that we wrestle not against flesh and blood.

On one occasion they returned to find that their gardens had been raided. Knowing that visitors often moved in to claim our time and trade goods in their absence, they laid the blame on Miguel's people, the village on the opposite side of the savannah, and invited them to a memorial feast to settle their differences.

The memorial celebrations were always a highlight in the social life of the village. The pulverized bones of the dead were saved for years, and once the death being remembered was far enough removed in time to have lost its sting, the occasions served for more than mourning. They sometimes included dancing, chanting, fighting, witchcraft, or carousing.

Guests were not always informed as to what was on the agenda, but Miguel's people had reason to suppose they would be called to task regarding the food that had been stolen. People in the Balafili valley were of the same opinion, and a group of men from Samuel's village came over to crash the party. When they had been working for Paul and Marty Shadle, a number of their possessions had been stolen by people from Miguel's village, and they were eager to register a public complaint.

The day of the celebration came, and Miguel's group filed into the village clearing to perform their colorful dances. They ate; they talked; they wept with those who sorrowed.

Darkness fell, and someone took up a chant of formal accusations against them. The charges were denied in a ritual response, and Miguel took the opportunity to air a few grievances of his own. The low murmur of chanting soon rose in a wild crescendo of shrieks and shouts as women from both sides began hurling insults back and forth, and the men of Samuel's village decided it was time to get into the act.

They stomped into the village clearing with bows and arrows, poles and machetes, and added their complaints to the din. The commotion was soon out of control. They would have to forgo their chanting and resolve their resentments a different way.

"Right here! Right here!" José began to shout, shoving the crowd back until they formed a circle around him. "Come right here, all you who've been talking about me!" He braced himself in the middle of the clearing, shoulders erect, chest thrust forward, feet placed firmly apart for maximum support. "Right here!" he yelled, slapping himself on the side of his chest to invite a test of his strength and endurance.

Before long there were two men dealing alternate blows to one another with clenched fists in the circle of wildly shouting spectators. Each tried to knock the other off his feet. Friends and relatives of both were yelling encouragement and offering themselves as replacements.

Accusations and arguments multiplied, and one of the men who had replaced the original opponents suggested that his challenger strike him with the broadside of a machete. So the contest progressed from fists to machetes, and then to axes.

They vented their angry frustrations throughout the night, and in the dawn of the following day the visitors gathered their

The Battle Begins

belongings together and stalked indignantly from the village. The party was over.

I shared their exhaustion. The tumult in the village had kept us awake most of the night and mocked us with the futility of our ambitions. It had been a year and a half since we had first tried to introduce the Prince of Peace to the big savannah, but it seemed that the same battles raged. What could we hope to accomplish between enemy villages, in view of the frail friendships that existed between *peaceful* groups?

The raiders struck again, wounding two young teenagers. As soon as the boys were strong enough to travel, the village was deserted for two months.

Not a wisp of smoke rose from the roundhouse the morning of their exodus. Not a sound broke the stillness. I leaned against the window and stared absently toward the empty village, wondering if everyone was safe.

I thought of the babies who had been fevered the night before and wondered if they were sheltered from the rain that was falling in the valley. I wondered about the cripples who would be crawling through the tangled, overgrown trails that were traveled in times of danger. The children would soon be crying in hunger. The women would be cross. The men would be on edge.

I turned away from the window and tried to concentrate on breakfast, but the hopelessness of the whole situation seemed overwhelming. I thought of the agony of Scar Shoulder's death, and of the identical piercing wail that must have risen from the enemy village when his death was avenged. How quickly our hopes for peace had crumbled! How absurd it seemed to expect any change! The ancient, bloody traditions of the big savannah seemed as unconquerable as the mountains that surrounded it.

I leafed through the pages of Isaiah's prophecy, and my eyes came to rest on a startling relevant admonition in Isaiah 43:19-21, "Remember ye not the former things, neither consider the things of old. Behold, I will do a new thing." And as an extra confirmation, "This people have I formed for myself; they shall show forth my praise."

It was an encouragement I was going to need. The situation was to get worse before it got better.

Visitors were coming. They had sent a representative a week earlier to ask José if he would assure them a friendly reception, and their proposed visit had been discussed with great excitement. It had been years since any of the Shamatali people had set foot on the big savannah, and great pains were now taken to provide a welcome worthy of the occasion.

A history of warfare had long ago severed relationships between the people of the big savannah and the Shamatali villages to the south of us. Only José's family had maintained a sporadic contact with relatives who lived on the fringe of Shamatali territory. But the aggressors in the original battles were dead and gone now, and the Shamatali offer of renewed friendship was heralded with wild enthusiasm. No bitter memories were going to mar the dignity of their return.

We sat by José's hearth and talked with his stepmother, a wrinkled old native of the Shamatali village soon to be arriving. She had been expecting her kinfolk for two days already, and her shelter was well stocked with garden produce. José had returned from a quick hunt, and was hanging chunks of smoked anteater over the campfires. Clothing, knives, machetes, and arrows had been set aside as gifts, and baskets of red seed pods had been collected to ensure that everyone would be appropriately decorated when the big day arrived.

The old woman reached for a roasted plantain from the embers of her fire, and with a hungry squawk her little green parrot sidestepped down the hammock ropes. "Are they coming now? Coming now? Coming now?" the old woman asked, mimicking its call.

The little green prophet ruffled its feathers. "Coming now! Coming now! Squawk!" it said, loudly and clearly to the old woman's ears. She fanned the campfire by her feet and settled back to wait.

The Battle Begins

The Shamatali people arrived in all their glory and congregated in front of our house to organize themselves for a colorful entrance to the village. They were beautifully decorated with white beads and brilliant feathers. Careful designs had been painted all over their bodies.

We hurried outside to meet them, buy many had never seen outsiders before, and they found the encounter more than just a little frightening. The women were greatly relieved when the leader of the party announced that they were ready to continue to the village.

They collected their belongings and had just started down the trail when one of the men stopped abruptly. "Oh! I was going to ask you about something," he said, returning to whisper into Wally's face. "Is it true that there's a God up there? Have you seen Him? Is He friendly?" The others hurried back to listen. They had often puzzled over the strange concepts José's family spoke of during their occasional visits to the home of their Shamatali relatives.

"It's true," Wally nodded. "I know Him inside me."

They held a hurried consultation among themselves. "Is it true that He's going to judge the world? Are we going to be caught in a fire? Us? And our dogs?"

"People who trust Jesus will be saved," Wally told them. "God doesn't want you to perish that way. That's why He sent us to warn you." They nodded their heads, and Wally continued. "The paper says that God's going to make a new earth—one where there's no sickness or fighting."

"And no snakes, either!" one of them added. They had heard that story before. The spokesman waved his arm in a wide circle that included the whole group. "We trust Him. All of us do. You tell Him that."

Some were impatient to get to the village, so they once more headed for the trail. "We're coming back tomorrow!" they shouted over their shoulder. "We'll sit with you tomorrow and you can tell us all you know about God!" We nodded and looked at one another, dumbfounded. That was quite an order!

Treasures of Darkness

We settled for two Bible stories. We would give them the account of creation, to introduce them to the Lord, and the story of the two ways, so they would realize that their final destiny depended on personal decisions. We realized that their background of scriptural truth was practically nonexistent, and we were depending heavily on help from our own villagers to fill in the blanks for them as the meeting proceeded.

All day long, different ones from José's family stopped by to give excited accounts of the visiting and to tell us that the next day they would be coming for a big meeting in which they wanted the Shamatali people to hear everything. José was coming, too. He may have had no interest in the message, but he surely enjoyed the prestige of owning some outsiders.

The following afternoon hundreds of people milled around the house, wondering how to squeeze into our little porch. José began directing traffic. "Women first! Women first! Go and call the women! We men go in later, when they're through! Call for the women!"

A few children ran to the edge of the woods, and shouted into the jungles where the visitors had erected temporary shelters. Our porch was soon crammed with seventy-five women and children who listened with puzzled expressions to songs and stories that left them completely baffled. Then they ducked out the door as quickly as they could to make room for the men, who had been shouting for them to hurry up. When the last woman had disappeared around the corner of the house, the men crowded in.

They stepped cautiously, picking their way across the floor littered with sticks, leaves, stones, firewood, dried wads of tobacco, and bits of crumpled paper the women had left behind. "Dirty women! Dirty, loudmouthed women! Where is there a clean place to sit?"

One of them eyed a bench suspiciously. "Did those women sit here?" He brushed it off with his hand, and still unconvinced that it met with his sanitary standards, he decided to squat on it. The others followed his example, climbing on the benches and squatting on their haunches to await the beginning of their first

The Battle Begins

"church service."

Their hosts had provided a background of information, and after singing a couple of songs, they turned their attention to the chart on the wall. They wanted to listen to the paper. Gradually their eyes focused on the drawings before them.

"That's a person! That's a bow and arrow!" they began to exclaim excitedly. "They're crouching as they walk along!" One of them lifted the corner of the chart and peeked behind it to see where the people were coming from. "They're stalking something! No–their faces are black! They're raiders waiting in ambush!"

They recognized each scene–people fighting, stealing, working witchcraft, capturing women. They enjoyed it immensely, until they discovered that all those people were on the wrong road.

Soberly they listened to an explanation of the narrow way. Those who walked toward heaven were God's children, and He protected them. They trusted Him like a child trusts his father. They tried to please Him. Their sins were forgiven, and their hearts were not burdened with guilt. They prayed for each other, calling down God's blessing and care for their family and friends. Their fear of witchcraft was gone.

When the meeting was over, the Shamatali men filed out silently, wondering whether or not the outsiders really knew what they were talking about. Could God really protect people? Could He take away guilt? Was He really trustworthy? Or should they warn their friends against accepting such radical ideas?

They returned to hear more, and listened intently. Not even José's jokes could distract them. They lost their nervousness around us, and we began to develop some definite friendships. They started spending time with us in the porch, and a young man we called Bad Eye became what seemed a permanent fixture.

"I'd really like this shirt," he said to Wally, hugging him tightly while he fingered the material he so admired. "Brother," he smiled, "if you only lived closer to me, I'd heap your table with deer meat, pig meat, wild turkeys, and fish! I'd really be generous!"

"Little One," Wally countered, "if you'd only heap my table with all that meat, I'd fill your baskets with axes, cooking pots, thread,

Treasures of Darkness

matches, and clothing! I'd really be generous!" Then he made Bad Eye a serious offer. "Listen. If you really want trade goods, help Paul build his house. We need ten hardwood poles."

Bad Eye pondered the offer thoughtfully. "Where's Paul?"

They walked over to the construction site of Paul and Marty Shadle's new home. "Brother," Bad Eye grinned nervously as they joined Paul, "maybe I won't, after all. The jungles are dangerous. Who knows where the raiders might be hiding?"

"Hoh," Wally answered, "OK." He was reluctant to send Bad Eye into the woods anyhow. He explained his hesitancy to Paul, but Bad Eye was tempted to think the shirt might be worth the risk.

"How many poles would you need?" he asked Paul. "Just ten?"

Paul Shadle nodded hesitantly. He was not sure the poles were worth the gamble. "Aren't you afraid?" he asked. Bad Eye studied Paul soberly.

"Would you avenge me if I were killed on the job?"

Paul shook his head. The price was getting too high. Bad Eye laughed with relief and decided he did not need a shirt. "Let's sit down and talk instead," he suggested. "Some other day I'll work for a shirt. Let's just listen to the paper today."

The following morning, the Shamatali visitors scattered in various directions. Some went hunting with José's group. Some went to Timoteo's garden to bring in stalks of plantains. Some went with David.

Bad Eye and his brother followed a group of women to Enrique's garden, where they hoped to harvest some taro. They hurried along the jungle trail in single file, watching for birds to shoot along the way.

The old woman in front of Bad Eye's brother disappeared over the crest of a hill, and he quickened his pace. Then a barely audible click behind him froze him to the core. He turned instinctively at the sound of a loud whisper. "Child, where are you going?" But before he could locate the speaker, an arrow had struck him in the eye and he dropped to the earth with a scream and a thud. His body shuddered under the impact of a volley of arrows.

The others rushed toward him at the sound of his scream, and

The Battle Begins

found him dead on the trail.

"Raiders! Raiders!" The cry went out again and was relayed to the village, where word soon passed around that the Shamatali visit had met with sudden disaster. He had been mistaken by an ambush party as a member of the village on the big savannah.

The old woman who had walked in front of him hoisted the lifeless form onto her back and carried him home, crying as she went. The others walked beside her, faces turned to the heavens, and wept bitterly. "Oh, my brother! My brother! Whatever will become of us without you!"

They reached the roundhouse and laid him gently in his hammock. They crowded around, calling to him, touching him, pulling hysterically on his arms, but to no avail. A search party hunted in vain for the raiders, and finally returned at dusk to join the village in mourning.

The next morning wood was gathered once more for a funeral fire, and Bad Eye's brother was cast into the hungry flames. His friends and relatives danced mournfully around the fire. His expectant wife wept brokenheartedly, and his little girl stood silently at her mother's side, not fully aware of the tragedy around her.

Wally and Paul went down to the village as the body was burning. They entered through the opening on the opposite side and slowly made their way around the circle of shelters, stopping here and there to talk with the others. "Children, sit down," the older men would say, in an attempt to prevent their going closer. Then they would grunt their assent as Wally explained that he and Paul had come to mourn with their friends.

Bad Eye saw them approaching and walked slowly toward them, holding up one shaky finger. He spoke with a voice that was strained and hoarse. "Just one," he whispered. "Just one. I'm just going to kill one of them."

A host of pat answers raced through Wally's mind. All of them seemed irrelevant. He could not tell the trembling man before him to leave justice in the hands of the law. There *was* no law. He could not say that it did not matter. There was no consolation.

Treasures of Darkness

Wally shook his head in sorrow "They've killed my friend," he whispered. "My own good friend. Yesterday he traded with me, and now he's gone. His slayers are obviously traveling the broad way that leads to destruction."

Bad Eye found the idea grimly appealing. He nodded his agreement and cursed them with a passion.

"And you, Little One," Wally added quietly. "Are you going to walk their way, too?"

He could not reply. The words stuck in his throat. But his eyes pleaded for understanding as he raised one quivering finger. Just one.

Two moons had died since the Shamatali visit had been interrupted by enemy arrows. Derek had made a routine visit to the Balafili valley, and had just been back a day or so when two young men from a village he had visited appeared at his door in a state of great agitation. They were part of the group that sympathized with the enemy village, and nothing but a dire emergency could have coaxed them to the big savannah. Fortunately, they arrived in the early dawn before our regular visitors began dropping in.

They hurried in to Derek's house, panic-stricken at the thought that someone might discover them there, and they struggled with their natural inhibitions against sharing family grief with strangers. The mother of one had been bitten by a poisonous snake the day before, and they were desperate for help.

Derek brought them to our house. He was still aching from his previous trip over the mountains, and thought Wally might be able to make better time on an emergency mission. The two boys watched them anxiously as they talked back and forth. They smiled with relief as Wally began to pack his medical supplies.

They started for the Balafili valley in a light drizzle, and though the trip did not promise to be enjoyable, Wally was confident that it offered an opportunity we had been seeking: a chance to win the confidence of a village that had been adamantly unreceptive to all overtures of friendship.

The Battle Begins

It was our second recent opportunity to spend extra time with the Balafili people. Just two weeks earlier, Samuel's group had set up temporary shelters in the jungle between their village and ours, and had sent a guide over to see if we would like to join them there for a couple of days' feasting on meat and wild honey.

Happy with the prospect of a brief vacation, we had accepted and were soon on our way across the savannah to the jungle resort that awaited us. Wally followed the same route now, hurrying behind his two young guides. Their previous urgency was gone. Wally was with them, and they knew everything would be all right. They talked and laughed, only sobering occasionally to ask Wally if he thought the woman would still be conscious.

They crossed a little stream and climbed a knoll to the area where we had camped with Samuel's people. Wally looked through the trees, smiling at the remembrance of our weary arrival. It had been the first time the children and I had accompanied him on the trail, and it had not been easy. The blue haze that marked their camping site had welcomed us with all the cozy promise of a light in a cottage window. But today's arrival was going to be different.

Our shelter had not been completed when we arrive, but Samuel had shown us grandly to our suite. "This is it!" he had said, waving his arms vaguely toward four lonely poles someone had stuck into the ground. "Hang up your hammocks!" There had been no roof over our heads and no walls around us, but our enthusiastic hosts had compensated by starting a roaring fire in the center of our "house" and crowding around to make us feel welcome.

"Samuel," Wally said, swinging in his hammock and studying the gray sky above, "why doesn't my house have any leaves over it?"

Samuel shifted closer, crooning as he would to soothe a child. "Little One," he laughed gently, "it won't rain. It never rains this time of year."

"Well *your* shelter has leaves."

"That's to keep the heat out," Samuel assured him with a faint smile.

"Well *we* don't want to get hot either!" Wally shouted in mock

Treasures of Darkness

annoyance, jumping up and waving his arms while he loudly reminded everyone of their promise to have a shelter ready for us. The men laughingly restrained him and offered assurances that everything would soon be taken care of.

No sooner had our shelter been roofed than a light sprinkle of rain began to fall. The men shuffled closer to the fire. Samuel stuck his finger out from under the eaves until it was wet, and then tasted it, licking his lips. "I wonder what this is falling from the sky," he mused. "It can't be rain this time of year. Why, it's honey!" He laughed and grabbed Wally by the shoulders, shaking him until he almost fell out of his hammock. "Did you hear that?!" he teased. "We told you this was a good area for honey! It falls right out of the sky!"

The daylight hours had been filled with friendly chatter, and in the evening the conversation had always turned to deeper things.

Wally's mind came back to the present while he followed his guides across a shaky pole bridge. The Lord was good. Perhaps the woman's condition had been exaggerated. Maybe her injury was just a divinely appointed mishap designed to provide an entrance to the village. They started up another mountain, and his mind wandered back to the evenings we had spent with Samuel's people.

They had wanted to learn new hymns. They had wanted to hear favorite Bible stories. They had wanted their questions answered. Could God really help people? Could He do things? Could He heal? Could He change the course of the wind or keep away the rain? Was He interested in their dogs, too, and their babies?

"Brother," one of the men had whispered, "does God know Clacamani? Do you?" They all hushed and inched closer.

Wally said *he* did not know him, but God certainly did.

"Clacamani's not a friend," Samuel whispered. "He's mean. He's an enemy of all Yanoamö. Just like Wacaboli."

"Wally," another interrupted, "didn't you say once that there is salt water between this land and your country?"

"Yes. So much you can't see the opposite shore."

"And nobody can drink it?"

"No."

The Battle Begins

"Brother, we think Clacamani did that. That's the way he is."

We began to realize we were discussing personalities in the spirit world, and soon they were asking if God knew *all* the spirits. Did He know the ones who sent fevers? Did He know the spirits of darkness? What about the ones that killed children? Was He aware of the ones that terrorized men and that paralyzed women? Did He know the spirits that tormented apprentice witchdoctors and sliced their souls with knives?

Wally assured them that God was fully aware of every spirit that existed, and they settled back with happy relief. They had been fully persuaded that God *intended* to make a new world for them that was free of spirit oppression, but they had always entertained an uneasy fear that perhaps God did not realize how difficult the job was really going to be.

One of Wally's guides interrupted his reverie by pointing to a thin column of smoke that rose from the jungles on the far side of the rolling plain. They were nearing their destination, and Wally was jolted from the past to the present.

The boys became tense as they approached the village. They stopped talking and listened intently for the sound of wailing that would tell them they had arrived too late. Death came quickly with a snakebite, and they had already been gone about fifteen hours.

They walked into the village clearing and were quickly ushered to the section where the woman lie. A man chanted mournfully beside her hammock. Leaves that had been used to sweep the ground and retrieve her spirit were scattered nearby, and the area was soaked with water that had been poured over her in frantic attempts to relieve the pain.

She was lying in her hammock, and the children around her were chased away as Wally approached. His heart sank as he realized the gravity of her condition. She had been bitten twice in the right arm, and half her body was swollen grotesquely. Her breathing was rapid, and she constantly moistened her lips with her tongue. She acknowledged his presence with glazed eyes.

Wally squatted beside her hammock and opened his medical kit mechanically. The hopelessness he felt was aggravated by the relief

Treasures of Darkness

on the faces of those who crowded around in eager anticipation of a miracle. Nothing short of a miracle would help. Her treatment should have been begun fifteen hours earlier and should have been three times stronger; but our supply of antivenin had been depleted by a rash of snake bites, and the nearest pharmacy was hundreds of air miles away.

He gave her a test to make sure she would not react to the medication and then proceeded with the injections. They asked if she would get better, and he said he hoped so. Nothing about her condition gave room for optimism, but he knew that the Lord had taken him there for a purpose. Her healing could be an inroad to the entire area. It could even mark a turning point in our dealings with the enemy village just beyond the mountains.

A crowd of people pressed around his hammock to listen to stories of creation and the way of salvation. They tried to sing a few songs. They studied the Bible story pictures he had taken along. They asked what it would be like in heaven. And they watched the woman beside them for some sign of recovery.

Three hours passed.

Darkness fell, and Wally got out a flashlight to examine her condition. She was not improving at all. They swung his hammock beside her, and he settled back to watch her in the flickering light of the campfire. Her breathing seemed more rapid, but there was nothing he could do.

Her husband hovered by her side, answering her in her delirium. Then the rhythm of her breathing stopped. So did Wally's. Her husband whispered Wally's name, and he moved quickly to her side. But there was no way he could help her. The woman's husband watched Wally closely, hoping desperately for a word of encouragement. When he realized that Wally had given up, he retrained his emotions only long enough to cry out, "An enemy has done this to make me sad! I've been defeated!"

His anguished cry brought the village to her side, and Wally sat back in his hammock, surrounded by their grief.

The night passed slowly, and Wally felt the suffocating throb of their hopelessness. "Little One! Answer me! Don't make me cry

The Battle Begins

this way! It's me–your cousin!" Then a piercing, forlorn wail rang out. "Wife! Speak to me! Mother of my children! What will I do without you? No young girl can ever please me as you did!"

Someone crouched beside Wally's hammock and whispered through the darkness. "Wally, will she get up again now? Is her spirit going to turn back and enter her body once more? Is God going to give us back our happiness again?"

"It's over," Wally said. "She's gone."

As dawn broke, the tumult became an indescribable agony. They knew the time was near when she would be swept away forever in the funeral fire. With trembling hands they placed leaves over her eyes and tied them securely with vine. They kept darting worried glances toward Wally, not wanting to offend him by dismissing him, but reluctant to share their misery with an outsider.

An old man finally approached him and squatted to the ground beside his hammock. "Little One," he said to Wally, "are you leaving now? Do you want a guide?"

The return trip was tedious and slow. They plodded heavily up and down the mountains. Wally relived the events of the night before and wondered what purpose it could possibly have. A dull ache pounded relentlessly in his head, and the grief-stricken words of the dead woman's husband hammered in his heart. *An enemy has done this to make me sad. I've been defeated.*

By the time he arrived on the big savannah, the result of his trip was written clearly on his face, and the people politely refrained from asking any questions.

5

Something New

The people that walked in darkness have seen a great light.

Isaiah 9:2

The Christmas season brought a startling change of attitude on the big savannah that bewildered us so completely we were scarcely able to receive it. An exuberant group aligned themselves with Enrique and decided to trust the Lord for time and eternity. There was no natural explanation of their sudden decision, and we hardly dared believe it was real. But they set themselves to the unlikely task of convincing us that they were really sincere. It was not an easy chore, and they tackled it with admirable optimism.

We had guarded against premature assumptions that their faith was real, but our skepticism faded under their cheerful insistence that they really belonged to the Lord. We began to share in their excitement. They settled securely into a new patience about the war, trusting themselves to their heavenly Father, and letting their anger melt in the warmth of God's love.

We decided to take them at their word and teach them accordingly. Because so many continued to give us their requests to be passed on to God, Wally and Derek decided to begin with an explanation of prayer. The doubts we still harbored were evident in that we announced an *evening* prayer meeting, knowing that none but the most sincere would brave the darkness for such a cause.

It was New Year's Day. We had been advertising the proposed prayer meeting all week and enjoying an enthusiastic response.

Something New

Enrique, David, and a few other former witchdoctors who had undergone torturous experiences in previous struggles to communicate with the spirit world had awaited the day with sober expectancy. In the same way that a witchdoctor had once helped them make contact with the spirits of the mountains, Derek and Wally were going to put them in touch with the Lord. Once they knew how to communicate with Him, they would be able to resume a cherished responsibility they had lost when they had severed connections with the spirit world. They would be able to intercede for their people.

The others, who had long ago resigned themselves to the fact that they would never be of intercessory value, were delighted to be included in the meeting. The very thought of learning to communicate directly with the Lord seemed to stagger their imagination.

The first arrivals appeared with the last rays of setting sun and others followed along in the darkness with glowing firebrands swinging at their sides. They were more than an hour early, and they settled down in the porch to while away the minutes with lighthearted banter that occasionally broke into peals of laughter. Every now and then they would exhaust themselves and sit in silence, until someone would lean over the partition to ask if it was nearly time.

Derek and Wally joined them, and everyone grew quiet with nervous anticipation. They gave undivided attention to explanations of how Jesus had taught His disciples to pray and how He wants us to bring Him our requests, our problems, and our thanksgiving. Through faith in Christ, God accepts us as His children and encourages us to speak with Him as boldly as a child talks with his father.

Then they began.

Derek prayed, thanking God for the earth and everything in it. He thanked Him that Jesus came to earth to save people from destruction and praised Him for the many of the big savannah who had come to put their trust in Him. "That's all," he said in closing. Nodding to David, who sat beside him, he whispered, "You're next."

David began to pray, faltering a little as he struggled to remember everything Derek had said. He tried to say he was glad that Jesus had come to earth but he did not feel comfortable using Jesus' proper name. It did not seem respectful. A few of the others snickered, and David quickly rephrased his words, changing "Jesus" to "Your Son." A relationship term seemed much more appropriate.

"Hnnnn, hnnnn!" Enrique murmured, encouraging him quietly.

David's prayer took on a more indigenous format, and he was soon talking comfortably with his Father, apologizing for having never spoken before.

"Father, God," Enrique began, as David finished praying, "I'm a descendant of Adam, and a friend of Derek and Wally. They tell us You like us and that You sent Your Son to earth to save us from hell. He was high up there with You, powerful and eternal, but He wasn't afraid to come down and become one of us. He didn't turn back, not even when He realized they'd kill Him."

He asked the Lord to take away his sin and to keep his heart set steadfastly on heaven. He presented his mother, his sisters, his brothers, and all his relatives to the Lord, asking His blessing on each one in turn. When he finished and his younger brother beside him hesitated nervously, he said, "Don't be afraid. God isn't frightening. Go ahead and talk! Go ahead! Your fear will disappear as you begin!"

His brother prayed, and on around the circle of men all but two took their turns. I could scarcely contain the joy that flooded my heart. We were one in Christ! It was real! The Light of the world had penetrated the darkness of the big savannah!

Once the circle was completed and Wally had finished praying, everyone straightened up and smiled in satisfaction at one another. Their decisions had been sealed.

History had been made. People from neighboring villages came to inquire whether the Yanoamö had really been communicating with God. When they heard the story affirmed, they looked at one another in pleased amazement. Few of them doubted God's power,

Something New

but never in their wildest dreams had they imagined that personal contact with such a One would be possible.

Curiosity brought even the most dubious to the following meetings. José occasionally sat in the circle of men that were beginning to pray with great enthusiasm and inventiveness, and his presence did not deter them in the least from praying as they always did. "Help José," they would say. "He's so stubborn! I've told him so often that You're really there, and he won't believe me. But help him in spite of that. Take away his sin and give him a peaceful heart toward everyone. He's always trying to lead us back into warfare, but we're not willing anymore."

They saw little results of those prayers, and José began to shout insults at them as they would leave the village for the regular meetings that followed. "Go and pray by yourselves!" he would hoot derisively. "I'm not coming! You're all being deceived! It's going to kill you yet! Don't say I didn't warn you! Ah!"

José never realized how greatly his warnings bothered them, because he was never around to witness the panicky discussions that followed such outbursts. They were well aware of the fact that they were treading a new way that had never been proved by their fathers, and they could not help wondering what complications might be hidden in the future. But neither did they realize the effect their new faith was having on José.

He sat in the porch with a visitor from Samuel's village, and I could not help overhearing their strange conversation. "Do they really communicate with God?" the visitor asked. "Even though they're still Yanoamö?"

José's answers were very quiet, and he appeared embarrassed to be caught in the uncomfortable position of having to explain the faith he derided. The visitor seemed excited with the prospects of prayer, and for some reason he seemed to take it for granted that José was counted among the believers. It was equally strange that José did not bother to correct him.

The weekly prayer meetings stirred both interest and dismay among the surrounding villages, while everyone watched apprehensively for the hidden dangers such a revolutionary practice might carry for the participants. But for the ones who had abandoned themselves wholeheartedly to the new way, the big test came one evening while Paul Shadle was visiting the roundhouse.

A loud commotion on the opposite side of the village climaxed in hysterical screams, and running across the clearing, Paul found Enrique's seven-year-old son unconscious. No one seemed sure of what had happened, and while some screamed that he was being strangled by spirits, others supposed that something had lodged in his throat. Enrique was alternately shaking the limp little form and pounding on the boy's back, but to no avail.

Paul shouted above the tumult, telling Enrique to carry him quickly to our house, and before long a loud wailing reached our ears as they hurried down the trail. We ran outside to meet them, and Enrique tremblingly held forth the body of his son in silent plea for a miracle.

Paul quickly explained how he had discovered him, and while Wally held the child upside down, Paul tried to dislodge the offending obstruction with some sharp slaps between the shoulder blades. But he had no success. There was no sign of life.

Stretching him out on the ground, Paul began to give artificial respiration. The people were beside themselves, trying to cooperate with us but fearing that every second was taking their little one further down the road of no return. I ran to call Derek and Jill, and we moved the operations into the porch.

We tried to think of some logical procedure, but our helplessness was painfully obvious to everyone. Enrique grabbed his son back to himself, hugging him desperately. He was hysterical with grief and fear. He shook his little one violently; he slapped and squeezed, and he rubbed the motionless chest in vain attempts to stir up some sign of life. Filled with panic, he began to wonder why he had ever dismissed the spirits who had indwelt him in the days of his witchcraft.

Derek turned aside to Wally. "We've been telling them God answers prayer," he said quietly. "We're going to have to show them. We're going to have to put ourselves out on a limb and trust God to do something." We all nodded soberly. We knew he was

Something New

right, but it seemed like a very shaky limb.

Wally, Paul, and Derek gathered around Enrique, squatting on the floor. "Let's tell God," Derek suggested gently, and once again a desperate father yielded his son. They stretched him out before them, and laying their hands on the still, small body, they began to petition the Lord for his life, asking Him to raise the child up like He used to do when He walked on earth.

Enrique relaxed his hold on the boy and waited for God to do something.

I hurried to the radio set and tried to find someone on the frequency who could offer some advice. Just as I was making contact with a doctor who "happened" to be visiting one of the other mission stations, Jill rushed in praising the Lord that the boy had suddenly begun to cry.

Enrique clutched him to himself at the first sign of life, and the boy promptly lapsed into unconsciousness again. But his breathing continued steadily.

In accordance with the doctor's instructions, we wrapped the boy in blankets and laid him face down on the floor with his feet elevated. It was torture for the weeping relatives–especially Enrique–to see him lying on the floor with no one doing anything. He so desperately wanted to hold him in his arms! He squatted beside him, propped his elbows on his knees and covered his face with his hands. There was nothing to do but wait and pray.

Enrique's wife came in quietly and sat behind her husband on a bench. She burst into tears at the sight of her son lying prostrate on the floor. I slid over beside her, wondering how to comfort her. "He's breathing now," I said.

She nodded, asking if we had told God about it yet.

"Yes," I whispered. "He's already spoken." I was referring to Derek's having spoken to the Lord, but she interpreted it to mean that God had already spoken on the subject.

"Oh!" she exclaimed. "What did He say?" And though I tried to set the record straight, others were interrupting to tell of our radio contact with the doctor, and she ended up with the firm conviction that we had been talking with the Lord by radio.

Treasures of Darkness

In an hour or so the boy opened his eyes. Derek looked to Enrique's wife and whispered, "Your son is looking for you." She did not hear him. A numbing grief had robbed her of her comprehension. Then she opened her eyes wide in bewilderment.

"My boy?" she asked. "My boy here? Has he returned?"

Derek nodded, and she slipped quickly from the bench and sat at her little one's head. He looked into her eyes, gazed with deep contentment on her tearstained face, and smiled wearily.

After he had been conscious for a while, the initial tension relaxed, and the crying gave way to loud scolding. Enrique and his family began accusing one another of having given the child a piece of meat too large to swallow. We breathed a sigh of relief. The din of accusations was very comforting. Everything was back to normal.

An hour passed, and when the boy sat up with no ill effects, we gave them an old blanket for the trip home. But bundled as he was in such an awkward position, they hardly knew how to transport him. Derek finally offered his services, and taking their precious cargo in his arms, he followed them down the trail to the village. Then they began to pray with loud, happy voices, praising the Lord for all He had done.

The story spread quickly across the mountains, and people in many villages pondered the effectiveness of prayer. It seemed that God was really dependable in a crisis.

The next few months swept by in a series of trials that threatened to overwhelm us. The new thing the Lord was doing did not go uncontested by the one who had enjoyed sole authority over the people on the big savannah, and the reality of the spiritual battle we had set our hands to came into grim focus. Recurring health problems forced Derek and Jill to take an early furlough, and we were left hopelessly handicapped in the daily routine of literacy, Bible teaching, medical work, visitation, and translation.

Medical emergencies commanded our time, and an epidemic of polio drained our energies physically and emotionally as we fought for lives we had come to hold very, very dear. José and Timoteo took advantage of a second memorial feast for Scar Shoulder to try

Something New

to stir up interest in continuing the warfare. There were cases of infanticide as unwanted babies were dealt with in traditional style. Violent arguments threatened to split the village. The spirits that at one time had controlled the affairs of the group returned in the darkness to torment the new believers. Night after night, Octavio would cry out in fear, and the men would rush to his side to claim the Lord's protection on his behalf.

But the spirit of the Lord was still at work, and His goodness could be traced through the difficulties. More and more joined the ranks of those who had planted their feet firmly on the narrow way. Several boys were now able to read and write. Paul and Marty Shadle gradually filled the gap left by Hadleys, and there seemed to be growing optimism that the Lord was able to protect the people on the big savannah from enemy attack.

I sat at the table with Ramón and Eladio, two young teenagers who often helped prepare literacy materials, and we discussed various methods of obtaining meat from the jungle. Anteaters were clubbed, snakes were impaled, frogs were skinned, monkeys were shot, and bee larvae were chopped from trees.

"Armadillos are smoked out of a hole," Ramón grinned. "Or drowned, if they live near the water." He held his hands to the sides of his head in imitation of armadillo ears. "They've got big ears," he laughed. "Just like new babies!"

"That's because babies turn into armadillos if they're strangled," Eladio laughed, leaning forward to further my education. "That's what we always say when we're joking. If a mother kills her newborn baby and throws it into a hole, it turns into an armadillo!"

Before we had time to continue, the front door opened slowly and José walked in. He held forth a trembling hand and told us he had just been bitten by a snake.

Wally pushed back quickly from the desk and grabbed José tightly by the wrist while we examined two punctures on his fingers. He had been bitten by a large bushmaster about ten minutes earlier. Wally put a steadying hand on his shoulder and led him to the porch where he settled down on a bench. He leaned

Treasures of Darkness

forward and rested his elbow on his knees, covering his face with his good hand while he awaited treatment.

I ran for the medicine chest, handed Wally the snakebite kit, and returned to the porch to offer José a little moral support. He had broken into a cold sweat, and his breath came in low moans. Ramón and Eladio raced over to the Shadle's house to call for Paul, and while he and Wally began to review the instructions that came with the antivenin, a crowd of curious onlookers collected in the porch.

José bore the pain well, but his initial groans grew to loud cries as the throbbing, burning pain in his hand ran up his arm and spread through his body. His vision blurred, his legs went numb, and waves of nausea swept over him. He felt as if his head were splitting in two.

José's mother came in crying and sat on the floor at his feet. Laughing Lady and Crooked Tooth were close behind. When they saw the fang marks on his finger and realized the size of the snake that had left two imprints an inch apart, they broke into a hopeless wail.

Once the initial requirements of the treatment had been completed, the women led José to the village. Wally and Paul visited him there three hours later to see if more medication was necessary.

His arm was swollen to the shoulder, and his skin was taut and fevered. His mother stopped crying long enough to ask Wally and Paul if they would pray for him, and since José offered no objections, they asked the Lord to protect him. They continued with the second stage of the treatment and left him for the night.

The following morning, small black spots appeared around the tip of the wounded finger. Wally rummaged through his medical kit, and José asked in a whisper if we thought the finger would rot off. We said it would not, but we did not speak with much conviction.

The women congregated around us to ask for prayer again. I looked at José to see how he would react to the suggestion, but his face was a blank. After we had both taken his needs to the Lord

Something New

again, José's mother decided that she would pray, too. "Father," she began cautiously, "my dear Father. This is the old woman speaking. I talked to You once before–You probably remember me. This man is mine. He's my own son, and he's in such pain! Who is there that can help us except You? The spirits have deceived us over and over. We would have trusted You sooner, but we didn't know You were there. Don't let my child be finished off this way! Heal him quickly so I won't be hungry! Heal him so I won't be sad and lonely. He plants my garden and shoots my meat. He makes me laugh when I'm bad tempered. What would become of me without him?"

When we were about to go, the old woman asked if she ought to fix her son some muddy water to drink. A certain type of clay, prepared according to specification, had always been highly praised for its healing virtues, though we had never been able to fathom its supposed effect.

"Why do you want to do that?" Wally asked. "Is it something the spirits taught you long ago?"

"No," she laughed. "They didn't tell us about that. We just like to do it because we think it will make him stronger. It's not good to drink ordinary water when you're injured like this." She sensed our uncertainty. "Does God say we shouldn't do that?"

Wally shrugged. "God never said anything about drinking muddy water," he laughed. "I won't tell you not to do it. But I don't think it helps much."

We told them we would be back the following day, and José mumbled something we decided to interpret as "thank you."

A few days later José came to the house by himself, walking with the aid of a crutch. He was weak and thin, but he seemed to be in good spirits. The swelling had gone down considerably, but the pain was still there, and his hand was terribly swollen and ugly. Tiny holes had formed around the bite, and they oozed constantly. The black spot had spread around his finger in ominous warning of trouble ahead.

Marty and I went to the porch to teach him how to soak his finger in a salt solution. "I don't want women witchdoctors," he yelled. "Where are the men?" Then he saw Wally and called out to him gruffly. "Brother! Come here and sit by me. Come and pray for me again."

He began coming every afternoon, and he did not seem to mind his female doctors once he recovered from the shock. In fact, he seemed to enjoy it so much we began treating him with more indifference than we actually felt.

He spent long hours sitting with Wally, discussing the reality of the Lord. José was confident that God would not harm him or allow him to go to hell, because He had already proved His love by protecting him from a close call with death. Wally would explain that God was prolonging his life to give him a chance to accept the Gospel, and though José often seemed to long for the assurance of salvation God had granted the others, he would remember his enemies and his eyes would harden. He could not afford to accept the Gospel. He could not afford the risk that God would take away his hatred for the enemy village. He did not *want* to lose that hatred.

The women arrived for a regular afternoon meeting while José was in the porch soaking his finger one day, and he left to wait outside. All of them prayed for him, thanking God that his life had been spared, and asking that José be put on the narrow way. I got the impression that they thought God would answer their prayers in spite of José's unwillingness to cooperate, so when they finished praying I tried to broach the subject.

"If José doesn't ask the Lord to cleanse his heart in the blood of Jesus, God can't put him on the narrow way. God isn't going to force him to be a Christian if he doesn't want to be."

"God can't put him on the narrow way!" Laughing Lady mocked disgustedly. "José's going to hell. Hell! HELL! That's what you always say!" She jerked her head in anger and laughed with a little embarrassment to see José standing in the door trying to find out why his name was being used so frequently.

She leaned forward and grabbed my arm. "Now tell him what you said," she said sarcastically, as he walked into the porch and squatted on the floor beside her. "Tell him God's going to send him to hell!"

"It's not *God* that wants him to go to hell," I replied indignantly. "God is offering him a way to *heaven*. If God had wanted him to go to hell He never would have saved his life."

José shuffled closer to us and watched me with narrowed eyes. Laughing Lady reached out and patted his arm gently. "Child," she whispered, "tell Margarita that you're not going to shoot anyone anymore. Tell her you're going to be a Christian. Tell her you used to say God was a liar, but that you don't talk that way anymore. Tell her."

But José never spoke. He fingered his sore hand, studying the blackening tip of his finger. He surely was not going to be shooting anyone with a hand like that. Laughing Lady watched him sympathetically, then turned back to me.

"Margarita," she pleaded, "don't make him sad. Tell him he's on the narrow road."

I shrugged my shoulders helplessly. *I* could not decide the man's destiny. She reached for José's arm and whispered to him urgently. "You *do* want the Lord, don't you?" Silently she begged him for an answer, just a short yes. But his only reply was a long, honest silence.

The men gathered for prayer one evening, and Enrique complained that his relatives in a village many days' travel to the north had no way of knowing that God was really there. "I always pray for them," he sighed. "And I ask God to turn them toward heaven. But how can He?" He gestured hopelessly toward Wally. "*You'd* never make it," he said. "You'd never be able to get that far."

"Well, *you* can go and tell people, too," Wally answered, mildly annoyed that Enrique should resign himself so quickly to his relatives' fate. The men all stared at him as though they could not believe their ears. They shuffled closer, smiling in anticipation as they asked him to repeat what he had said.

"You men can take the Gospel," Wally repeated, looking from one startled face to another. "Just as God sent me here to teach you, He can send you forth to share with others."

"Wally," Enrique grinned, "do you mean me? I'm still a

Treasures of Darkness

Yanoamö! Would God send me, a Yanoamö, with His message?"

Wally said He would, and Enrique turned to his brothers with happy excitement. "My brother Wally says God wants me to go and teach others," he chuckled. "He's saying that I can go with the Gospel just like he came here to bring it to us!"

The others smiled their congratulations. "Really?" one of the more doubtful asked, with a hand on Wally's arm. "Really? Can *we* go, and tell people the Lord sent us?"

Before long they were enthusiastically subdividing their world and setting forth areas of responsibility. "I can go to the people beyond the western ridge," Octavio volunteered. "My wife has relatives there. They'd accept me."

"That's right, that's right!" Enrique nodded. "That's the way we need to do it. And the northern villages can be mine. It's a long, hard trip, and Wally would never make it over the mountains. If the outsiders want to help, they can take the message to the enemy village. We're too scared to go there, anyway."

Once their plans had been made to everyone's satisfaction, they straightened up, surveyed the circle of men who had met for prayer, and decided it was time to begin.

They prayed with fresh enthusiasm, asking the Lord to send them out, just as He had sent the outsiders to the big savannah. "Father, God," one of them rejoiced, "all of us are going to follow Your narrow path! All of us! If You send us to other villages, none of our people will be left behind when You return for us! We'll all be together! Even the old women!"

José was not there that night, but two of his brothers were among the group. As their turn came to pray, they asked the Lord to put them on the narrow way. "Father, our brother is deceitful," one of them apologized. "But don't hold that against the rest of us. Take away our sin anyway. We'll follow along Your way without him."

"That's the way!" the others whispered, in recognition of the painful decision they had made to leave their brother behind. "That's the way!"

Once the circle had been completed, Enrique offered the closing prayer. "Father, I was in darkness," he concluded. "And I didn't realize I was sitting on the brink of hell. But now there's a brightness in my heart. There's a star shining in the darkness, and it grows brighter all the time. I'm beginning to see."

Timoteo and José came in a few days later with a group of their relatives and waited for everyone to leave so they could talk with Wally alone. They called him to the porch and motioned him to a bench.

José was the spokesman. He squatted before Wally, and leaned his elbows against Wally's knees. He shuffled back and forth, trying to find a comfortable position, and shifted his wad of tobacco nervously from one side of his mouth to the other. "Brother," he began, smiling a little self-consciously as his brothers prodded him to tell his tale, "something happened yesterday.

"I was out trying to hunt," he said, flexing his fingers a little, and frowning at the black-tipped finger that still would not bend. "And I was all by myself near the north savannah." He changed his position a few more times. "The ground started shaking, and I did not know what to do," he said, hesitating again until Wally nodded his encouragement. "I stood still. I looked high up in the trees. They were shaking all over! They sounded like they were falling apart! Branches were breaking off and falling around me."

He paused a moment, and beads of perspiration formed on his brow. "Brother," he continued, holding tightly to Wally's arm, "I looked up at the sky, and it was shaking, too. I looked down at the ground, and it trembled. I was terrified! I always thought I was fearless, but I turned and ran to the village as fast as I could. I got into my hammock and stayed there quietly until my chest stopped pounding.

"Finally I told the others what had happened, and they said it must have been God." He stopped, waiting for Wally to deny it. "They're lying, aren't they?" José asked. "Brother–Wally–Was it really God? Could He do something like that?"

"Yes, He could," Wally nodded, a little puzzled over the strange tale. José was not given to hallucinations, and earth tremors were relatively common to the area, but no one else had reported a similar experience that day. Maybe there *had* been a local tremor, just for José. "The world is in His control," Wally said. "It *must* have been Him."

They all began to talk at once. José's brothers tried to convince him that God was really powerful and that all the things people were saying about Him were true. Timoteo stood to one side, strangely quiet. He and José had always been together on major issues, and it puzzled him to see José so preoccupied with spiritual concepts. Perhaps the Gospel really did have something worthy of consideration.

Never had José been so intrigued with a discussion of God's claim on him. He was desperately interested in finding answers to the questions that plagued him. "Brother," he said, once the initial flow of conversation began to slow down again, "why would God do that to me? Why does He want to scare me?" For a man who had just endured a serious snake bite and his own personal earthquake, it seemed a very relevant question.

"I suppose He wants you to know He's really there," Wally said. José was delighted.

"He really wants me, doesn't He!" He smiled pensively.

A number of men decided to set out for distant villages where they had once enjoyed friendly relationships, to share the Gospel with friends and relatives long forgotten. Enrique and his brothers collected an assortment of Bible story pictures and songbooks and left for a group of villages four days' journey to the north. Others revived an acquaintance with villages scattered beyond the western range, and José's relatives spread the Word among the Shamatali people, who had not returned since the slaying of Bad Eye's brother. The fact that the Yanoamö were making direct contact with the living God was big news, and before long the Shamatali people announced their intention of paying another visit to the big savannah.

Once their official entry was over and the gala reception past, they set up a temporary camp in the jungles behind our house, and the captain paid us a formal visit.

Handsomely attired in a green shirt that he must have acquired

Something New

through trade with a downriver group, he strode confidently into the porch and carefully leaned his bow and arrows against the wall. Silently he studied the interior of our home and ignored my greeting.

"Woman," he finally said, impatiently deciding to recognize my humble presence, "call your man. I want to speak with him."

Obediently I called my man, and he joined the captain in the porch.

"Brother," the captain began, "I want to bring all my people to learn now. We want to hear everything you've been telling the people on the big savannah. Why should *we* remain ignorant of something like this? We want to know how to pray." And before Wally could answer, the captain scanned the porch with a frown and demanded to know where everyone would sit.

Wally started to tell him that the meetings would begin a little later. As their presence was discovered in the porch, an inquisitive crowd collected to join the discussion. A few of José's relatives tried to interrupt Green Shirt to explain how things were planned, with children's meeting first, then women, then men. But the captain waved them to silence and they backed off, giggling at one another to see how forcibly he attempted to reorganize the customary schedule.

"Brother," one of José's kin explained, "we never come *this* early. The outsiders blow a horn when they're ready to begin."

Green Shirt stared him to scorn, and turned back to Wally. "We're ready right now," he declared grandly. "Blow the horn!"

"OK," Wally laughed, enjoying such a rare show of authority. I hurried off to see if Paul and Marty were game to start the afternoon session earlier than scheduled.

Paul stepped outside and blew a loud blast on his trumpet, calling forth a crowd of children from the roundhouse. They raced down the path, burst into the porch, and pushed toward the benches, while Green Shirt stared incredulously at the sudden invasion of "his" meeting.

He started shoving them out the door, and José's relatives burst into delighted laughter at the growing confusion as Wally tried to intercede on behalf of the bewildered students. "Shamatali! Stop!" Wally laughed. "We've always taught the children first! That's why they came when they heard the horn! Why don't you wait outside until they're done with their class?"

Green Shirt could not believe the indignity he was being called upon to suffer. "My people are already here," he argued. "We're already waiting!" He gestured toward the crowd swarming around the house. The women were sitting on a scattering of poles in the yard, and the men who were not already in the porch were milling around the door trying to squeeze in.

"Wally," one of José's brothers whispered, shaking Wally by the arm, "send the children back. They won't mind. Let's just teach the visitors today." The students nodded their assent. Nobody wanted to upset the guests. They quickly relinquished their prime time for a good cause and were relieved to no longer be a point of contention. They wiggled through the crowd and disappeared out the door, hollering last minute instructions over their shoulders for Wally and Paul to "tell them good"!

Green Shirt organized rows of people all over the floor, and once he was satisfied that all was well, he nodded for Wally and Paul to begin. Paul taught them a few easy choruses, and while Wally explained a passage of Scripture relating to eternal life, Green Shirt stood up to reinforce the teaching by adding explanations after each sentence. When the meeting was over, he organized an exodus of the men and called for the women to come in and sit down quietly. We were beginning to wish he would stay permanently.

When the final meeting came to a close, Enrique's mother followed Marty and me to the little dispensary and asked for an antiasthmatic pill for Ramón, one of the young teenagers who had been helping us compose new literacy material. "If only his brother were here," she sighed, referring to Enrique, who still had not returned from his trip to the northern villages. "If only my son were here to pray for him."

We assured her that the Lord heard everyone's prayers. Nodding sadly, she wrapped Ramón's tablet in a wide leaf, tied it neatly with

Something New

a vine, and hung the little packet around her neck. "Little One," she whispered, hanging on my arm for a moment, "you outsiders pray for him, too. He can't sleep well."

The following day we canceled our usual schedule and decided to take advantage of the Shamatali visitors' interest by putting ourselves at their disposal to teach them as long as they were willing to learn. A midmorning meeting continued into the afternoon, and would probably have carried on till sundown if we had not been interrupted by David and his cousin shouting urgently at the front door.

They were as pale as ghosts, and their eyes were filled with terror. "The boy with the big chest," they whispered, desperately trying to say with their eyes what they did not want to form with their mouths. "Our little one–the one that was sick–he's finished."

My throat constricted. *Not Ramón!* His life was just beginning, and his love for the Lord was just starting to blossom! It couldn't be! He studied with Paul every afternoon. He sat across the table from me every morning. How could he be dead? But it had to be him. Chronic asthma had given him a barrel chest that was not proportionate to his size. I formed his name silently, and David nodded.

Wally grabbed his medical kit and tore down the path to the roundhouse, shouting over his shoulder for me to send Paul. But they arrived too late. The boy had been found dead in his hammock, and he apparently had died in his sleep while his family was working in their garden. No one had been aware of the gravity of his condition, and they had left him to guard the house, but the little guard had fallen into everlasting sleep.

A crowd had gathered around him, and they backed away to let Wally and Paul examine him. José was standing nearby, straight and tall, with his bow and arrows clasped formally to his side. He began an impassioned chant as they approached him. "Here you are! Here you are at last! Raise him up! Bring him back! Let's see God make him live again like you promised! You're the ones who say we don't need witchcraft. You're the ones who say God will take care of us. Hurry up! Let's see if your word is true! The people are crying already. Bring him back to life now!"

Wally and Paul returned a while later, and the Shamatali visitors who had been quietly talking by the house quickly picked up the baskets, bows, and arrows, and retreated respectfully to their encampment. Marty and I listened to the men's description of the situation and decided to go down to the village for one last look at our little friend.

The reality of his death sank in as we neared the roundhouse and heard the sound of the wailing. We picked our way over the debris surrounding the village and entered a door near Enrique's section. Screams and shouts pierced the air, and a few children silently motioned us to the area where the crowd had gathered.

Enrique's sister, Doré, was dancing a slow, mournful step near the family shelter. She waved Ramón's shirt in the air, and held up the small black trousers I had given him the week before in appreciation of his help with the literacy stories. She wailed in utter abandonment, and I took it for granted that she was chanting, until Mary whispered in amazement that she was *praying*.

We paused to listen and cringed at the honesty of her prayer as she poured out her disappointment to the Lord. "Father, God! You told us You'd help us! What have You done? We believed You! You promised protection, but our little one is gone! Why didn't You heal him? Whatever will become of us in our sorrow? Oh!"

I could not bear to look at her. I pushed through the throng for a closer glimpse of Ramón, while Marty stopped to talk with some women sitting on the edge of the crowd.

I reached his hammock and crouched beside him. His mother was on the opposite side, frantically calling to him as she hovered over his lifeless form. "Child!" she pleaded. "Little One! Come back! Answer me!" But there was no response.

I shared her agony. He did not *look* dead. Death was cold and hard, but he was still warm and natural. He *couldn't* be dead! He looked better than I had seen him for a long time. His breath was not coming in gasps, and his chest was not heaving anymore. He was motionless. Too motionless.

Something New

His mother flung herself into his hammock and hugged him fiercely. She shook him by the arms. She turned his face toward her. "Little One!" she wept. "Wake up!"

I studied his face and swallowed hard as memories of other days flashed through my mind. I reached out hesitantly and touched his arm, his chest, his face. *Wake up!* I echoed silently, begging for a response. I stroked his hair, and the women sitting beside me stopped crying to see what I was going to do. It dawned on me suddenly that they thought I was working to perform a miracle.

I stared at them incredulously for a long moment, then wilted with the hopelessness of it all. How could they expect me to raise the dead? I turned away and wept in helpless frustration.

We started back home and met Eldona at the door of the roundhouse. "Can't you do anything?" she whispered.

We shook our heads.

"But we'll see him again when Jesus comes," Marty said.

Eldona frowned and jerked her head in slight annoyance, studying us with puzzled eyes. Were we making fun of something so serious? Had she really heard us correctly? David's wife joined us and looked inquisitively at Eldona.

"She said they'll see him again," Eldona explained hesitantly. David's wife studied us silently and pouted. Marty and I looked at one another blankly. Why should we have a hard time explaining such a concept? Ever since we had first told them the gospel, we had taught of the hope of eternal life.

David's wife grabbed Marty by the arm. "*Is* that what you said?" she demanded. "Are you going to see him again?

"Yes," Marty answered cautiously. "And so will you."

Eldona motioned excitedly for a few others to join us. "They say they're going to see him again!" she whispered, laughing breathlessly as she allowed herself the luxury of half believing us. It did not take long for a crowd to gather.

"Are we saying something wrong?" I whispered to Marty. We were thoroughly confused that they all seemed to think we were teaching a new idea. One of the women tugged at us excitedly.

"Come on over and tell the old women!" she suggested, leading

Treasures of Darkness

us to José's section. She shoved us under the leaves into a smoky shelter, and an old lady sat up in her hammock as we stumbled unceremoniously onto her hearth. She pointed with her chin to Ramón's house.

"Have you been sitting over there?" she asked. We nodded, uncertain as to how we were to proceed. Laughing Lady and her daughter stepped over the tangle of hammocks to join us.

"What were you telling those women?" she asked.

"We told them we would see the boy again," I said.

They looked at one another, smiled, and moved a little closer. "What did you say? Are you going to see him again?"

We nodded.

"Ugh! I'd be afraid! Aren't you afraid of ghosts?"

"We won't see him as a ghost," we explained, still puzzled over the strange reactions. "We'll see him just as he was. Only without asthma."

They looked incredulously at one another.

"That's what we've always told you," I said. "After a Christian dies he goes to be with God."

"Little One," Laughing Lady whispered, putting a hand on my arm, "you said they go to be with Him, but you didn't say we would see them again. That's frightening! Will we really see him?"

"It's just like it was with Lazarus," Marty said. "When Jesus called him back to life his sisters weren't afraid of him, were they? Why should you be afraid?"

They looked at one another in astonishment. "Will it really be like that? Will we see him like a person—not a ghost?"

The old woman leaned forward and delivered a stern warning. "Children, don't deceive people. Don't lie about things like that. Don't give people false hope." She stopped for a moment, undecided about her own opinion. "You *are* lying, aren't you?"

I shook my head numbly. I was not lying. But the intensity of their appeal for truth was overwhelming. Were we really willing to guarantee that a person who died would live again? *Lord*, I prayed, *it is true, isn't it?* They searched our faces for confirmation, and for a fleeting moment I struggled to lay hold of my own convictions. It *was* true. Death had been conquered.

"We're not deceiving you," I said. "God says that when Jesus returns, all those who have died in faith are going to be with Him in body. It's not a lie."

Laughing Lady's Fat Daughter jumped to her feet. "Well, then, go over there and tell them!" she laughed excitedly. "Don't leave them standing there crying in vain!"

She was not joking. We did not know what to do. Our prophecy had stirred such a dramatic response we really were not sure of the impressions we were giving. Nor did we have the nerve to interrupt their mourning with an announcement they might interpret as a command for Ramón to return from the dead right then and there.

"They're crying too hard," Marty finally answered. "We'll tell them when they come to our house."

"Do you expect *them* to go to your house?" the old woman snapped in exasperation. "Do sad people go visiting?"

Laughing Lady snorted her displeasure. People in mourning do not leave their hammocks for days. No one bothers them. They are left in respectful solitude until they feel like mixing again. She did not think much of our lack of concern. Why would we not tell them to stop crying? Why would we not tell them they would *see* him again?

"*You* tell them, then," I said. "You go over and tell them what we said. I'm afraid to. I'm afraid to approach people when they're crying like that." We got to our feet.

"Never mind," she muttered. "I'm scared, too."

We walked home quickly, wondering about the excitement we had left behind and wondering whether or not we should have interrupted the mourners.

We had not been home long before some men came down to the house. They were the same two who had come to announce Ramón's death earlier. They called for Wally, and asked what we had told the women in the village.

"They said that when Jesus comes back, the boy will be with Him—alive and well," Wally said.

The younger one was beside himself. His eyes were wild and his

Treasures of Darkness

voice trembled. "What do you mean?" he demanded shakily. "Will we see him like a ghost or like a person?"

"Like a person," Wally answered. "He *will* be a person. He'll be just like you and me—only he'll be indestructible. Eternal. Sickness will be unable to hurt him anymore."

"*See* him?" the young man continued, on the verge of hysteria. "We'll see him here? Among us? Right in our presence? Will we grab hold of him again? Will we touch him? Will I hold him and not let go? Like this?" He grabbed tightly to Wally's arms and shook him fiercely.

Wally looked at me quizzically. He was beginning to experience the same bewilderment Marty and I had felt in the village. He turned back to his inquisitor.

"Of course," Wally assured him. "You'll know him then as you knew him now. You'll see him, talk with him, live forever with him." The young man calmed down and looked to David for his opinion. Was he going to believe such a fantastic tale?

"Brother," David whispered, "is it really true? Will it be like Lazarus coming back to life when Jesus called him out of the cave?"

Wally nodded, and David said nothing for a few moments. He struggled for faith to believe that it was true. A pleasant spirit-realm had sounded like a lovely promise in comparison with the restless, cruel afterlife they had always envisioned, and the thought that eternity with the Lord offered a complete, happy life for real people was staggering.

Finally he nodded his head. It was true. "But today we're sad," he apologized, holding Wally's arm and searching his eyes for understanding. "Even in spite of all you say, we can't stop crying."

"We're sad, too," Wally nodded. "We cry even though we know we'll see him again someday."

David murmured his agreement. They stood silently for a few moments, and then the two men excused themselves and returned to the village.

Wally sat at the table and pondered their response to the news of eternal life. Did their hysterical excitement indicate that we were

Something New

not communicating properly, or had familiarity with doctrine dulled our own responses to the wonder of heaven and reduced a victorious hope to the level of cold theology?

It was a long, dreary day, and since the people kept to their hammocks, our house was empty at nightfall, and we decided to go to bed early. But we were still awake when a woman called softly at our window, asking to be let inside.

I fumbled for the door and admitted three women, barely distinguishable in the dim glow of their firebrands. I could scarcely believe my eyes as they slowly came into focus. It was Doré, who had been chanting her heartache to the Lord, with her mother and her sister. According to custom, they should have been home crying for their little one. They, of all people, should never have left the village to discuss their loss with outsiders.

"Sit down on the bench," I suggested. "You're all weary." They settled themselves quietly beside me, and after a moment the old woman spoke.

"Little One," she said, "is it true? What you've been telling people—is it really true?" My mind was whirling. Someone had found the courage I lacked and had given a ray of hope to Ramón's family.

"It's true," I said. "You're going to see him again. It's obvious that he belonged to the Lord. He's already with Jesus." They nodded silently, and I continued. "Don't think he's in his hammock, frustrated to be caught by death. That's just his body that was sick so often."

Doré nodded vigorously. "That's right," she agreed. "He's gone. He's not there." She reached out for my arm. "Jesus will come soon, won't He? That song we sing says He's coming soon."

"I don't know," I said. "Nobody knows how soon it will be. He's eternal. He's not in a hurry like we are." I was not too hopeful that she would understand. I was not sure I did either.

She began to cry softly, chanting another prayer. "Come back soon. Come back soon. We're lonely for our little one. Come back quickly. Brother, come soon!"

"I just want to ask one more question," the old woman

Treasures of Darkness

whispered, as Doré's chanting faded to a mournful hum. "If Jesus is going to bring him back to life, maybe I shouldn't burn the body. Maybe I should leave him in his hammock."

"You can burn him," I said, as gently as I could. "He's going to have a new body. A body that's strong and everlasting. Don't be afraid to burn the body in the hammock. It's empty."

She got to her feet, crying softly, and picked up the firebrand she had left by the door. "I keep wondering–" she began haltingly. "José says we shouldn't deceive ourselves. He says we'll never see him again. He says if God were faithful, He never would have let the boy die."

"Don't worry about what José says," I whispered. "He doesn't understand yet. God didn't say we would never get sick and die. He said the whole world is dying because of sin. But He promised we would live again if our hearts are clean."

"Margarita," Doré whispered, with one hand on the door. "What you say is true. We're going to see him again. God wouldn't deceive us. But right now we can't stop crying. We're overcome."

I murmured my understanding and wished I could tell them they were not as overcome as they thought they were. The hopeless finality of previous deaths was nowhere in sight. Death had lost its sting.

6

Ripples

Except a corn of wheat fall into the ground and die, it abideth alone: but if it die, it bringeth forth much fruit.

John 12:24

Like the ever-widening circle of ripples created by a pebble tossed into a stream, the effect of Ramón's death began to reach into the surrounding area. For the first few days following his death, our porch was crowded for impromptu sessions centering on the second coming of Christ. Both the Shadles and we were overwhelmed by the constant demand for meetings.

The Shamatali people struggled to unravel the mysterious message that had taken the hopelessness from death, and they found they could neither accept it nor ignore it. Balafili visitors arrived seeking verification of confusing rumors that had sifted through the jungles–rumors regarding a bodily resurrection of the dead. Then Miguel moved his people across the grasslands with the intention of camping nearby.

He arrived at noonday, directed a large company of friends and relatives into the porch, and seated them quietly on the floor.

"Brother! Wally!" he hollered over the partition. "We're all here! Women too! Come and talk with us! Tell us something!"

Wally joined them and surveyed the strangely subdued crowd that filled the room. Miguel grabbed him by the arm and pulled him down beside him on a bench. "Wally," he said, making a guarded reference to the boy's death, "tell us what's happening.

Treasures of Darkness

What are you saying to people?"

"Do you mean about the crying the other day?" Wally asked, politely avoiding the word *death*. They nodded their heads and shuffled closer.

"Wally," Miguel whispered urgently, "we really want to learn. Tell us everything. We're not going home until the Shamatali people leave. We're going to stay and join in the meetings with everyone else. We want to find the Lord."

They gave their undivided attention, concentrating on the message in a determined effort to understand, and interrupting Wally to ask all the questions that came to mind. Then Miguel suggested that Wally teach them to pray. They did not want to waste any more time. Their decisions were made, and they were anxious to seal their commitments with the words of their mouths. They bowed their heads, and one by one they introduced themselves to their Maker.

For three days, Miguel's village mingled with the others on the big savannah in a constant succession of meetings that left us pleasantly weary at the close of each day. But the tempo finally decelerated, and the normal routine of life took over. In one way or other, the compelling urgency for spiritual understanding was satisfied. In some lives the thirst for assurance of eternal life had been quenched by a personal acceptance of the Gospel, and in others it had been dulled by rejection.

Then the Shamatali visitors decided it was time to leave, and we were caught up once more in the hectic traditions of the big savannah. The Shamatali people had been camped nearby for a week and a half, and having depleted the local food supply, they found themselves faced with frequent suggestions that they soon return to their own village. Unwilling to be chased away like dogs, they attempted a dignified exit by challenging their hosts to a mock battle on the runway.

"A battle?" we asked, when David told us of their plans. "You're going to fight each other?" It did not strike us as a fitting conclusion to their visit. "God says you ought to treat your neighbors as friends."

Ripples

"We *are!*" he grinned. "We're not going to use bows and arrows!"

Preparations were fairly simple. The savannah grass grew in tangled clumps that pulled from the earth in one piece, making a solid clot of dirt and roots that was easy to handle and not too devastating to be hit with. The warriors ran through the long grass collecting their ammunition and depositing their haul on the sidelines, where the women and old men stood by watching. The children helped out wherever they could, and when the stockpile was considered sufficient, the battle began.

They divided their forces into two groups, one large and one small. The larger division took on the "home team," and the smaller one tackled the men from Miguel's village. The lines were ill defined, but there was a semblance of order, with the small teams engaged in hearty warfare at one end of the battlefield, and the large teams heaving artillery at one another on the opposite side. They were matched in pairs, and only occasionally would someone step aside to help avenge a hit that had slammed into a relative. Then he would resume his own private battle.

The shouts and screams could be heard all over the savannah, and it was not long before the whole village had arrived to take part either by fighting, collecting clumps of dirt, screaming encouragement, or guarding ammunition piles. Others who could not work up an enthusiasm for the Shamatali farewell squatted on the sidelines and watched the proceedings with passive indifference.

Some of the spectators started to shout back and forth. The good fighters and the poorer ones were becoming evident, and a general attack was launched against the agile ones who so far had managed to avoid being hit. "Get that one! Get that one!" the old men screamed to their younger relatives, wildly pointing out the victims of their choice. "Nobody's ever hit him yet!"

"No! Not that one!" others would yell. "He's already been hurt twice! Get the other one!" Tempers flared, and even the crowds on the sidelines began screaming at one another.

Green Shirt stepped in and called a halt. Some followed him to the side of the field, and other continued with the fight. A few hot-tempered Shamatali youths shouted their demands for a continuation of the contest with blunted arrows, but the older men on both sides decided they had better quit while they were still friends.

The children spent half an hour clearing the debris from the runway, and after everyone had drifted back to his own home, Enrique wandered to the porch by himself. It was his first appearance since he had returned from the northern villages to find his little brother gone, and his face was still streaked with tears.

He sat with Wally on a bench, and no one spoke for a moment. "You know," he finally began, "I've been sad." He leaned forward and rested his arms on his knees, studying the floor between his feet. "I just can't be happy. I can't pray."

"We're praying for you," Wally assured him. "God's going to make your heart strong again. He won't desert you."

There was a heavy silence for a moment before Wally continued. "Enrique. Have the others talked with you? Did they tell you you'll see him again?"

He studied Wally's face carefully, then nodded. "So it's true? How soon will Jesus come back with him?"

"It might be a long time," Wally said. "You might be lonely for a long, long time. But it's true."

"You're right," he sighed. "I know it's true. When I think of heaven, my sorrow leaves in spite of my desire to be sad." He rested his head wearily in his hands. "Some people thought I'd stop following the Lord," he commented. "Some people thought I'd be so angry I'd never pray again." He shook his head slowly as though he could not quite understand their logic. "How could I do that?" he wondered. "Where would I ever find another like Him?"

Samuel arrived from the Balafili valley and stopped by the house before he hurried on to the village. "Wally! Where are you?" he shouted over the partition. "It's me! I've arrived! Come quickly! I'm in a hurry and it's getting dark!" Then while he awaited Wally's arrival, he untied the package that hung around his neck and

Ripples

pulled out a little can of money.

Pausing only long enough to exchange exuberant hugs with Wally, he dumped his few coins onto the partition. "There!" he said, dividing them according to size. "That's all I have. Three baby coins and two mother ones. How many books can I buy?"

Wally reached for a stack of booklets from a shelf behind him and handed them over the partition. "Take whichever ones you like. You can have this many." He wiggled four fingers in front of Samuel's face.

Samuel nodded and leafed happily through the selection, choosing the Bible stories with which he was most familiar. His money would have purchased more than four, but we had learned the wisdom of always returning a little change. He invariably recalled his need of a few extra items before he returned to his own village.

Wally scooped up the coins and pocketed most of them. Actually, it was only a nominal fee for the booklets. A small charge ensured that we would not find crumpled paper scattered along the trails. "Here," Wally said, poking fun at the customary designation of large and small coins. "You can keep a mother one."

Samuel detected the smile in his voice and struggled to keep a straight face. "Just put her back in the can," he ordered soberly. "Maybe she'll have more babies." Then he leaned over the partition to reach the stack of books that had been replaced on the shelf. "Wally," he asked, "how much would it cost to buy all of these?"

"*All* of them?"

"We need everything you have," Samuel nodded. "Everybody's asking for them. We've already given away all we owned."

He proceeded to tell of seven villages he and his people had been visiting in a spontaneous effort to spread the gospel. They had even been traveling back to the enemy village where Samuel had taken Paul Dye and Wally, months earlier. "Sometimes we forget the words of the songs," he acknowledged. "But we just sing our own words." No one in his village was literate, but it did not seem to deter them in the least; they could follow the stories by studying the illustrations.

He read the interest that sparkled in Wally's eyes and responded with a typically boisterous description of their evangelistic efforts. "We get all dressed up," he laughed. "Beads, feathers, clothing." He pulled on an imaginary pair of pants, and adjusted an invisible hat. "Then we get a big stack of books, wrap them in banana leaves to keep them dry, and off we go to teach people all about God!"

"OK, OK," Wally smiled. "But what do you say when you get there?"

"We tell them everything you tell us!" Samuel laughed, as he adjusted the package on his back and gathered his bow and arrows together.

"I have to go now," he said. "It's dark. I'll be back in the morning."

"All right," Wally answered. "Go quickly."

Samuel spent the evening in Enrique's house, and the conversation around the campfires turned to the possibility of reaching the enemy village with the Gospel. The idea was surprisingly well received by people who not many moons earlier had been content to call fire down from heaven upon them. When Enrique and Juan realized that Samuel had already begun visiting that area with others from his village, they offered to accompany him on the next trip.

Not everyone received the proposal with equal enthusiasm. The women cried themselves to sleep, and Timoteo spent an exhausting evening trying to reason them out of such foolhardy plans. It was still under discussion the following morning when a group of them arrived at our house with Samuel to help him spend the rest of his money.

"I don't know," Samuel pondered, considering the responsibility that would be his if something went amiss when he arrived with them in enemy territory. "Maybe I should go back with my brothers a few more times before any of you accompany me. Maybe you shouldn't come over yet."

There followed a few moments of contemplative silence before Enrique answered. "All right," he agreed. "Go ahead without me. Maybe Wally will take me over with him later on."

Ripples

All eyes turned to Wally to see if he would be in agreement. He and Paul Shadle made regular monthly trips to the enemy village, but they had never considered so radical an idea as inviting someone from the big savannah to go with them. Wally was hesitant. He shared Samuel's uneasiness at the thought of assuming such a responsibility.

"What if they shot you?" Wally asked Enrique. "What would I tell your family when I returned without you?"

"What do you mean?" Enrique asked, a little puzzled. "I wouldn't stay dead forever, would I?"

"No, of course not. But people cry in loneliness."

"Yes, they'd cry all right," he acknowledged. "If you tell me not to go yet, I'll wait. But I'm not afraid to go. I'm not afraid to die. They can't destroy me eternally."

Samuel nodded, relieved that Enrique was willing to listen to advice. "Wait until later, then," he said. "We'll keep going by ourselves, and we'll convince them yet. We'll persist. They're already starting to be persuaded a little."

None of the others looked especially impressed by Samuel's final statement but Wally and I stared at one another incredulously. "Really?" Wally exclaimed, turning to Samuel. "What do they say?"

Samuel shrugged. "Oh, they say they'd like to be Christians and stop fighting."

"They're lying!" Timoteo hissed, leaning forward to affirm his convictions in Wally's face. "They'd *never* stop fighting!"

"*Are* they lying?" Wally asked Samuel.

"How should *I* know?" he answered blankly. No one could afford to get too excited over the possibility that it might be true. To let down their guard prematurely could be fatal.

José's finger was not improving. The blackened tip was rotting away, and José studied it with unease, wondering where it would end. When a visiting doctor examined it and suggested amputation, José did not object. He had seen the damage caused by other snake bites, and he was willing to give up a finger in order to save a hand. But he was relieved, nonetheless, when the doctor discovered he did not have his surgical equipment with him. José was given a week to make mental preparation for the ordeal, at which time the doctor would be returning with the necessary equipment.

Once we realized that the plane would be landing in a few days, Paul and Wally reviewed an idea they had often discussed, and they decided to check on the possibility of flying a few of the men out to visit a lowland base where the Gospel had already gained a solid foothold among a separate group of Yanoamö on the Padamo River. Joe and Millie Dawson, our co-workers in that area, asked the believers there if they would like to host such an expedition. They called us back on the two-way radio to report that the idea had been enthusiastically received.

Once the plans were rumored over the savannah, we could easily have filled a DC-3 with the applicants who earnestly pledged themselves to be Christians forever if we would just take them for a ride in the plane. Even José was willing to hazard such a promise for a thrill so prestigious!

Four men were selected for the dubious honor of flying out to visit a strange village: David, Enrique, David's older brother, and a representative of Miguel's village who had come to be known as Nice Guy. For a while they were torn between the pleasure of having been selected and the fear of accepting, but they soon decided to go, though it meant traveling in "outer space" to an unknown location where they would be at the mercy of strangers. That was no little consideration for people traditionally suspicious of everything new. Wally was to accompany them, and Paul would remain on the big savannah to assist the doctor we were expecting.

The families of the four men made feverish preparations. As the day approached, we were besieged by offers to do whatever jobs we could invent for them, in a concentrated effort to earn money, clothing, soap, and books so their kin would not appear "uncivilized" at the other end of their journey.

The plane arrived late one afternoon, and the following morning a crowd gathered while the sun was still low in the eastern sky. The relatives of the travelers were boisterously happy one minute, and grimly despondent the next. The trip sounded like fun, but who

Ripples

could tell what might happen? Maybe their men would die of fright in an airplane. Maybe planes were just built to accommodate outsiders. Or perhaps the lowland tribesmen would poison one of them. And what if the Padamo River people turned on them, taking advantage of the fact that they were so few in number?

About an hour before scheduled flight time, the four nervous astronauts filed down to the river with a bar of soap. The yard was overflowing with their friends and relatives. The older ones tearfully begged us to promise that all would be well, and the younger ones enthusiastically laid out new wardrobes on the grass.

The four well-scrubbed celebrities returned from the river and sat on poles to begin their meticulous preening. Wet hair was flattened down smoothly; earrings were adjusted; and beads, strings, shirts, and pants were put on with the help of the whole assembly. And finally they congregated in full splendor beside the little red plane.

"Ho! What will we do with our bows and arrows?" David demanded. "The plane looks too small."

Wally told them they would have to leave them behind, and the crowd was thrown into a mild frenzy while they discussed the alternatives.

"I'll run home and get you a machete!" a little boy shouted to one of them. "They're smaller!" The others scurried around begging and borrowing from the crowd. But David was not meeting with much success.

"Brother–Wally," he pleaded in desperation, "loan me a machete! I'll never ask again! What can I *do*? I can't arrive empty-handed!" So Wally loaned him a machete, and once they all had something firmly clasped in their hands, they squared their shoulders to face whatever might lie ahead.

Jim Hurd, our new pilot, gave the "all aboard," and the four climbed confidently into the plane. They soberly peered through the windows at their mournful relatives.

"Wally," Enrique whispered, "ask Jim if he put gas in. We don't want the plane to die of thirst while we're up there."

Jim assured him that all was well, finished his preflight check,

Treasures of Darkness

and climbed in. It was time to pray. All of us bowed our heads, and David asked the Lord to send away the wind and rain, and to keep the party safe. The door slammed shut, the propeller whirred into action, and soon they were roaring down the runway and lifting into the sky.

I had been giving my attention to Wally and the others in the plane, and I was not prepared for the sight I found as I turned back to the house. There was not a smiling face in sight. Young and old, men, women, and children alike were lined up along the house sobbing. David's father put a shaky hand on my shoulder to turn me around. "Child," he whispered through his tears, "will they befriend my sons? They won't start a fight, will they? Oh! I'm already sad and lonely!"

Once the crowd dispersed, we settled down to business in the dispensary. Paul and I worked as intermediaries between the doctor and José.

It didn't take long for José's relatives to congregate around the infirmary, where they availed themselves of the wide, screened windows that permitted a close study of the proceedings. They wept sympathetically as the doctor motioned José to move closer.

José took a chair across the table from the surgeon and held out a trembling hand for inspection. He was covered with a cold sweat. Paul and I moved in on either side of him to offer moral support. He winced as the doctor prodded the decaying flesh, and he watched apprehensively as an injection was prepared to deaden the area. A moment later the doctor tested the effectiveness of the injection with the point of his knife, and José hastened to assure him that he still felt the pain.

The doctor waited a moment and tried again, with the same results. "He doesn't feel anything," the doctor smiled, prodding a little deeper. "He's just frightened." The women at the window screamed in terror, and José fastened his eyes on the doctor's hand, steeling himself for torture.

Satisfied that the area was without feeling, the doctor opened a little case and selected a tiny, sharp knife. I looked over at Paul. What do we do now? José kept reminding us that his finger was

Ripples

not numb yet, and he was trembling so violently that he shook the two of us on either side.

The women began wailing a morbid description of all the doctor's cutting instruments, and José began to sway back and forth.

Suddenly, Laughing Lady burst through the door and rushed frantically toward us. The doctor ordered her outside, and as she was ushered back through the doorway she screamed, "Hold him tightly! Margarita! Hold him! He's going to die of fright! Paul! Hold my little one tightly!"

We took her advice and pressed against him from both sides, leaning firmly against his shoulders and holding his arms securely. He stopped trembling instantly. The doctor decided on the tool he wanted, checked to make sure the door had been locked, and bent over the outstretched hand on the table before him. Just as he cut into the finger, we covered José's eyes with our hands.

The women watched the doctor cut away the flesh from the bone, and screamed in alarm. Then the patient whispered, "Margarita, has he started yet?"

I breathed a sigh of relief. The doctor had been right. "Yes, He'll soon be done," I whispered. "Don't be frightened."

The doctor continued chipping away at the bone, and Paul watched the operation with all the eager enthusiasm of someone who thinks he may be called upon to perform a similar service someday. I could not be so objective.

"He's sewing it together now," I whispered a short time later.

Then it was over; the finger was thrown into the garbage, and the stump bound with sterile gauze. We removed our hands from José's eyes and let him have a look at the doctor's handiwork. H nodded numbly and turned away whispering that he did not feel good.

He was faint for half an hour, but once he managed to compose himself, he swallowed an aspirin and left for the village.

The following day the travelers returned, and a happy crowd surrounded them to hear the details of their visit. They were such assured men of the world, nonchalantly describing the people they had met and the places they had seen. No, of course they had not been frightened in the plane! Yes, of course they had been well received! Each had a box of gifts he had received from his hosts—food, arrow points, feathers. They handed them over to relatives who gladly carted them off to the village for inspection, and the travelers followed them down the trail describing the wonders of their experience. Their downriver counterparts had strange haircuts and adobe homes! They all wore clothing and tried to speak Spanish! They had built a school and bought guns for hunting!

But the full effect of the visit was yet to be felt. They pondered the things they had seen and heard. The lowland Yanoamö were ordinary people like themselves, but their way of life was remarkably free of witchcraft and warfare. Maybe such a change was really possible for the big savannah, too!

The village was astir with excitement. They had found a cause to embrace, a goal to pursue. The chance that they would ever have attained to a life-style like ours had never seemed remotely possible, but now they had discovered a realistic objective. They would adapt the new ways of their lowland kinsmen: *they* were real people!

Enrique began calling the people together at dusk each evening for prayer and song services, and before long they had devised a morning "pray around" as well. The first man awake would begin to chant a loud prayer from his hammock, and one by one the others would pray in turn around the circle of the village. The men began arranging occasional hunting expeditions to provide meat in quantities sufficient for community suppers like they had enjoyed downriver. When the time came for the annual rebuilding of the roundhouse, a few of the more adventurous men decided to build themselves four-walled dwellings.

Marty and I wandered into Enrique's shelter on an afternoon visit just as the men were returning from the jungles with hardwood poles for the new houses. They dropped them to the ground, and rubbing sore, stiff shoulders, they proudly pointed out the boundaries of the new, enlarged houses they were beginning to build.

Enrique's house was going to be built around the old shelter where they still lived, but it seemed to be about four times as large. "Who's going to live here?" I asked, in sudden dread of the sanitary horror that would be produced by cramming thirty or forty people inside those four walls.

"Just us," Enrique beamed.

"But it's so big!"

"Well, so is yours," he teased. "No. Look here. My wife and I will sleep in this section with the children, my brothers will sleep right here, and my mother and sister will swing their hammocks in that corner." He had indicated only half the available space.

"But who's going to sleep out here?" I asked, waving my arms around in a wide circle.

"That's not for sleeping," he laughed. "That's for praying. We never have enough room to sit in a circle and pray around in the evenings. We're too crowded. We need a special place to meet, like they have downriver."

I was stunned for a moment, and my brain struggled to interpret his idea into a concept I could grasp. "Marty!" I interrupted, rudely breaking into English. "Did you hear that? This is for meetings! It's a church! The first church they've ever had, built without our money, without our advice, and without our knowledge!" We looked at one another with an excitement Enrique could not understand, and he smiled at our enthusiasm.

The sounds of the joyful noise they were making unto the Lord often kept us awake in the night. In keeping with their customary exuberance, they squeezed every drop of enjoyment from their meetings. The continued enthusiasm on the part of men, women, and children finally aroused our curiosity so much we decided to go down to the village some night and investigate. We did not want to interfere in what the Lord was doing, or give the impression that our western traditions of worship were the ultimate, but who ever heard of prayer meetings being *that* exciting?

Treasures of Darkness

Wally and I made our way to the village one evening after supper, shining a flashlight along the path before us. We hurried down the path in single file, discussing how we would insist on keeping in the background once we arrived.

We need not have worried. Once we found our way to Enrique's house, we were vaguely directed to the back of the crowd in a dark corner. Someone motioned for me to sit down by a pile of banana skins that had not yet been thrown on the garbage heap behind the village. Wally was seated a little more prestigiously in a circle of men.

It was dark except for the glow of campfires, and one smoky corner of the house was designated for the women and children. The men formed what more or less resembled a circle, some squatting on the floor, some sitting on firewood, some lying in hammocks, and some leaning against the walls. People were still entering, and the crowd shuffled this way and that as everyone hunted for a place to perch.

In spite of the fact that we had determined to keep in the background, I almost felt miffed when David and Enrique consulted together without asking Wally's opinion and decided that the time had come to call the service to order. "Let's sing first," Enrique announced, and everyone looked to Pedro, who seemed to be the acknowledged song leader.

Pedro was swinging in a hammock hung high above the floor, with plenty of room for people to sit underneath. He cleared his throat and began the Yanoamö version of "Jesus Loves Me." The others joined in heartily, one at a time, each starting at the beginning of the song and singing in his own private key. The advantage of that system was that people who did not remember the words could wait until they heard someone else say them, and then follow along.

Before long, everyone was singing on a different line, and when Pedro completed the song and realized that no one else was finished, he started at the beginning again. The final outcome was that rather than deciding on a fixed number of verses to be sung, Pedro gave them a time limit. When he thought the song had

Ripples

continued long enough, he began clapping his hands. The ones around him followed suit, and when the hand clapping was heard in each corner of the house, the choir gradually faded away.

After three songs, someone decided it was time to pray. My back was beginning to get stiff so I inched backward, a little closer to the banana peelings, in an effort to rest against the wall. Then I discovered that I was sitting on the thruway used by cockroaches traveling to the garbage pile beside me. I had leaned my head against the wall, and was soon swatting at all the bugs whose route I had disrupted, clawing them frantically out of my hair while I hastily resumed my former position.

David began to pray in a loud voice, and the noisy hum of whispering women and children hushed so quickly it startled me. The women were not usually that attentive. My eyes grew accustomed to the darkness, and I stole a glance at the crowd. Women were squeezed together in two corners now, with small children and babies asleep in their laps. Only an occasional whisper or shuffling could be heard.

David praised the Lord for a number of things and asked His help concerning sickness, raiders, snakes, thorns, sick dogs, neighboring villages, unbelievers and the Derek Hadley family. From time to time the Hadleys had written reports of their progress in their battle with sickness, and we had always shared their letters with the group.

Then, though everyone was still bowed in prayer, David began addressing the congregation. "You who still bother the women, don't think that just because you happen to dream about God you're a Christian now. You become a Christian by asking Him to take away your sin! You know God when His Spirit indwells you, not when you dream about Him!" Then he returned to his prayer.

Others followed the same pattern, interrupting themselves from time to time with a few words of exhortation to suit the needs of specific problems. Everyone was thankful for the hope of eternal life, and many marveled that Jesus had been willing to come to earth in order to save mankind. Since Ramón's death, all eyes had been turned heavenward, and the more they thrilled with the

Treasures of Darkness

wonders of heaven, the more they stood in awe of the fact that Jesus had been willing to leave it all behind.

There were advantages to their ingenious system of prayer and preaching. Every head was bowed quietly, and all the fiery injunctions were accepted with no argument. It seemed to be taken for granted that any disagreements would have to be held in check until such times as the one with the contrary opinion took his turn in the circle of prayer.

Their prayers were peppered with remarks concerning not only the present and the future, but also the past. All the Bible stories they had ever learned were mentioned, and I began to realize why their memories seemed so exceptional. Each story was being taught over and over again in their meetings. "Father, God," one of the men prayed. "My children are sick. When You made this land You made it perfect, but Adam and his wife sinned and ruined everything. I wonder why Adam's wife was so stubborn. We don't imitate her ways. We imitate Noah. We would have been on the ark if we had been there in those days. We're certainly descended from Noah, not from the ones who drowned."

When the last man had prayed, they jumped to their feet and ran out the door. Wearily I began to get to my feet and stretch my aching muscles. Then Enrique called out, "OK, women! Come around now. You're next. Move into a circle and begin."

My heart sank with the realization that we were only half done, and I was relieved that the women were too tired to pray for very long. By nine o'clock the meeting was over, and the house was vacated except for Enrique's family.

"Enrique," Wally said, as we got to our feet, "is it always this crowded?"

"Sure," he chuckled, delighted with our surprise. "Every night!"

There was great excitement over the power of prayer. By then we had been on the big savannah for over two years, and deaths and illnesses had been reduced drastically. Yanoamö visitors always marveled at the abundance of children playing in the village clearing, and wondered at the good health everyone enjoyed. Our medicine could probably have claimed part of those results, but

Ripples

only the Lord could explain the sharp reduction in cases of snakebite and injury. The raiders were still known to make occasional ambush attempts, but no one had been shot for months. Considering the fact that five people had been killed or wounded during six short months of the previous year, that was quite a record!

It was Wednesday night, time for the weekly prayer meeting we still called in our porch, and we were not aware of the thrill the evening had in store. Pedro, the song leader, was first to arrive. He leaned over the partition for a friendly chat while we waited for the others to congregate.

"Did I look frightened the first time I prayed?" he grinned.

"No."

"Well I was," he laughed. "I was so scared my legs were trembling, and I thought my voice wouldn't make a sound!" He turned at the slam of the door and settled down beside the others to share happy recollections of their first prayer meeting.

The crowd was unusually large and included such improbable people as José and his brother. *Just what we need,* I thought, as he strutted across the porch with a wide grin. It would not have been the first time he had participated in a prayer meeting just for a good laugh. Once he had announced his intention of praying and had proceeded to thank the Lord for narcotics and witchcraft. Then he had burst into gales of laughter and said he had just been joking.

The meeting came to order, and one by one the men began to pray. When the man next to José finished, José shuffled into position and covered his face with his hands. I was almost afraid to listen.

"Father," he began hesitantly, "I've talked to You before. Sometimes I said I wanted You to take away my sin, but I was just lying."

I swallowed a lump in my throat and strained to hear every word he whispered. Could it be possible?"

"I didn't really want You to take away my anger. I wanted to kill people. Sometimes I said my anger was gone and that I didn't want to fight anymore, but that was a lie, too."

Everyone had been hushed, as if none could quite comprehend what was happening, but finally they began to murmur quiet encouragements as José continued.

"This time I'm going to tell You the truth, My heart is sinful, and I still want to fight. I want to kill. I didn't want anything to do with You at all, but Enrique keeps talking with me. He tells me I should be honest with You. I say I don't want to be a Christian, but I really *do* want to be Yours. I want to be happy and content like Enrique is. I want to know Your Spirit within me."

Lord, I whispered within myself, Lord! How can it be? How can You do such a thing! I could not have felt a greater awe had José's amputated finger suddenly grown back into place! I stole a glance at Wally, who was sitting silently in the circle of men with his head bowed. How could he sit there so calmly and serenely when I felt like jumping up and shouting?

"Take away my desire to kill," José continued. "Take away my anger and give me a peaceful heart."

On and on he went, discussing his past with the Lord. The men sitting around him grunted their approval of all he said, adding "Yes, that's right" at the appropriate places and reminding him of sins he had forgotten whenever it seemed that he was exhausting his memory. It was a cooperative venture to clean up one of the darkest corners of the village, and I felt a little of the rejoicing there must have been in the presence of the angels as José became a new creature.

7

The Long Road to Peace

When a man's ways please the Lord, he maketh even his enemies to be at peace with him.

Proverbs 16:7

José's long-awaited profession of faith fired everyone with fresh optimism that all things were really possible, and they began to ask the Lord for friendship with the enemy village.

But friendship, like charity, had to begin at home. The Lord began to focus their attention on their own unfriendly attitude toward the world around them, and they came to some discouraging conclusions. Not only did they harbor resentments against distant villages because of feuds dating back years before our arrival, but even their relationship with Miguel's village had scarcely progressed beyond mutual tolerance. Worse yet, situations had developed within the confines of their own village that made a mockery of their high ambitions. Friendship with their *enemies*? They could hardly maintain friendship with their friends!

The mass enthusiasm for Christian service that had highlighted their initial response to the gospel had begun to fade as some who had received the word with gladness fell into the category of those who endure but for a season. The leaders had resolved on behalf of the entire village to follow the Lord with all their hearts, and they found the lack of full cooperation extremely annoying. It was an insult to their authority. Theoretically they understood the principle involved in the parable of the sower and the seed, but

Treasures of Darkness

nothing could alleviate the frustration they felt. They could not tolerate indifference.

Woefully lacking in patience, and ignorant of spiritual growth, they attempted to intimidate everyone into conformity. Those guilty of sin, suspected of sin, or thought to entertain the possibility of sin all came under thundering condemnation. And the problem was compounded by the fact that their concept of sin was limited to the little they gleaned from Bible stories, plus a bewildering assortment of personal preferences. We suddenly had too many "babies" to care for properly, and were swamped by the simultaneous demands for Bible translation, literacy materials, and teaching outlines.

The nightly meetings that had once solidified their new unity in Christ became a battleground. False accusations met with hot denials, and attendance dwindled as various segments decided they would rather stay within the security of their own shelters and pray with their immediate families.

Enrique was completely disgusted with the whole village.

"*None* of them really want to follow the Lord," he grumbled, joining us in the porch and sitting dejectedly by the fire. "Just me. I'm just like Noah."

Wally slid over beside him to ask what was wrong.

"What's wrong?" Enrique echoed incredulously. "They all pretend they're innocent! I tell them to stop hiding their sin, and they get up and leave!" He snorted angrily. "I knew they were lying all along," he fumed, naming a few people he suspected of immorality. "And Catalina never stays home with her husband. She's always sitting by Antonio's hammock."

"Well, that's not everybody," Wally said, in an attempt to brighten the picture for him. "That's only five people you've mentioned so far. How's Pedro? How's David? What about Octavio? And José?"

"Yes–José!" Enrique muttered. "José and those liars from Miguel's village! They're always gossiping about me. How can anyone be sincere who insists on using tobacco? *I* tell them they'll all go to hell if they don't get rid of it, and then *you* tell them I'm lying!"

"I don't talk that way," Wally corrected him. "I just tell them the reason you say that is because you don't have a Bible in your own language. You teach what you think, instead of what you read. God never said people will go to hell if they don't get rid of their tobacco. He never mentions tobacco."

He glanced at Enrique, who was nodding glumly, and paused in frustration. How could Enrique be expected to know the Word? The Scripture portions translated into the lowland dialect were beyond his comprehension, and the passages we had translated into the local dialect were *nothing* compared to the bulk of Scripture yet undone. He turned back to Enrique. "Did I ever tell *you* that God wouldn't forgive your sins unless you quit using tobacco?"

"No," he admitted. "But if I don't say that, they'll never quit. *You* don't use it," he said defensively. "And neither do the people downriver."

"We don't *want* to," Wally explained. "I want to keep myself clean and healthy. But I don't pretend that God commands it or threatens us with hell. He *doesn't*."

Enrique sat in uncomfortable silence, resting his chin in his hands. "Listen, brother," Wally said, putting a comforting arm around his shoulder. "Don't be so discouraged. I know you want everyone to follow the Lord, but you have to be patient. Don't worry if some prefer traditional hairstyles. Don't be upset just because some like to paint their faces red. They don't have to turn into outsiders to be acceptable with the Lord. God *likes* Yanoamö."

Enrique murmured a dubious reply, and Wally racked his brain for something that would show Enrique the futility of his dogmatism. His eyes lit on the strand of beads around Enrique's neck. "Have I ever told you that God says your white beads are sinful?" Wally asked. Enrique looked up, startled, and fingered his necklace. "Maybe you just like drawing attention to yourself," Wally suggested with a faint smile. "Maybe you wear them because you like to flirt with the girls."

Enrique's face relaxed in a smile. He knew Wally was just

Treasures of Darkness

teasing–just trying to prove a point. "*I* don't flirt with anybody," he laughed. "Beads are OK–aren't they?"

"Sure they are," Wally chuckled. "God's concern is for your *heart*, not your outward appearance. What you need to do is teach people to respond to the Holy Spirit, and let *Him* guide them in those things. Just preach against the things He *does* condemn. Speak out against gossip, deceit, and immorality. Those are the things that will do real damage."

"I *do*," Enrique insisted. "I'm always accusing everybody of adultery, but no one will admit it."

"I know you are," Wally nodded, remembering the long line of complaints he had received from the others. "Maybe the problem is that you accuse *everyone* even though just a few are guilty. You can't condemn an entire family for the fault of one."

Enrique looked annoyed. "OK," he answered crisply. "I won't say anything. I'll move away and let them fend for themselves. You can take care of them."

"Ho! Is that what I said?" Wally asked. "God *wants* you to help each other. He *wants* you to warn people against sin and teach them His Word. Otherwise you'll end up fighting again. When you make sweeping accusations you can't prove, though, it's bound to cause arguments."

They sat in silence for a few moments before Enrique answered. "You're right," he sighed. "It's no good this way. My heart is restless all the time. My contentment is gone."

He returned to the village and brooded over his problem for a few days, refraining from outbursts that would aggravate the situation, but his annoyance was obvious to all who failed to measure up to expectations. Tension built to a precarious level and eventually erupted into a violent argument. It was Enrique who brought us the report.

"You remember how angry I was when Catalina kept sitting by Antonio's hammock?" he asked.

Wally nodded.

"I stayed angry," he admitted grimly. "And though I never said anything, my anger burned in my chest. She never returned to his hammock, but I kept thinking she really wanted to. I was sure she preferred Antonio to her husband.

"Then last night she came to the prayer meeting. It infuriated me to see her sitting there so innocently! I started shouting at her. I really lost my temper. She ran to her own shelter crying, and her uncle, Timoteo, jumped to her defense. He was afraid I would hit her with something.

"The two of us faced each other across the clearing and yelled back and forth, threatening one another like we used to do. We never did actually come to blows–just defiled our mouths with filthy words. Then we quit in exhaustion and returned to our own houses.

"The rest were continuing with the meeting, so I sat back in my hammock. But when it was my turn to pray, I discovered that I had no words. My mouth was empty and so was my heart. I'd been deserted. The Spirit had left me."

His voice shook as he continued. It was a memory he did not enjoy. "I was terrified. I stretched out in my hammock and wept. The women gathered around crying 'What will become of us? What will happen now that you've angered God's Spirit? Where will we ever find another Helper like Him?'

"We couldn't sleep. We mourned all night. Everyone came to see what was wrong, and when they realized I'd been deserted, they prayed for me. They put their hands on me, and asked the Lord to send back His Spirit. He finally did. He took away my guilt. He returned to my chest, and I could pray once more."

Beads of perspiration stood out on his forehead. He rubbed his hands slowly across his face, trying to erase the memory. Then he sighed deeply. "I still feel weak."

Enrique straightened up and managed a feeble grin. "Wally," he said, "it made me wiser. No more screaming and shouting. That's it."

They sat in silent contemplation for a few moments, each engrossed in his own interpretation of the event that had taken place. "You know," Wally finally said, "the Spirit didn't really leave you. He only–"

Treasures of Darkness

"He did! He did!" Enrique interrupted. "Brother—I know it! He was gone!" He clutched at his chest, remembering. "My heart was empty and lonely."

"He made you feel that loneliness so you'd repent," Wally explained. "That's how He coaxed you to be obedient. You silenced Him by your stubbornness, but He didn't *leave* you."

Enrique smiled tolerantly. He didn't want to argue the point. He'd had enough arguments for a long time. "Well, I'm all right now," he grinned. "I'm not alone anymore."

Wally and Paul called the men together to review the series of events that had led to the mystifying affair they had witnessed. They had all been shaken by Enrique's experience. No one, however resentful of undeserved criticism, had been unmoved by his despair.

They listened intently as Wally explained the development of their problem, showing how unresolved differences had led to suspicion, and on to gossip and false accusations. Personal grudges were forgotten as each began to recognize his own responsibility for the barriers that had come between them. Some began to acknowledge personal involvement in specific instances.

Enrique cleared his throat. "Some people think I was angry at everyone," he began. "I wasn't angry. If I'd been angry I wouldn't have said anything at all."

"That's right," José answered, with a faint smile that defied interpretation. "Angry people don't speak. They just lie in their hammocks and suck on tobacco leaves."

"No, of course I wasn't angry," Enrique continued. He squatted on the end of a pole, elbows propped on his knees and hands clasped together and pressed against his mouth. "It's just that I'm anxious for everyone to follow the Lord."

He paused for a moment, and the others squatting beside him murmured understanding. No one obliged him to continue, but he plunged ahead. "I don't have a Bible," he said. "So how do I know what God's Word says? I only know what my brother, Wally, tells me. Sometimes even though I think I know what He says, I'm mistaken."

The Long Road to Peace

"We're all that way," David sighed, whacking his machete into the pole beside him for extra emphasis. "I've tried to learn to read, but I still can't hear what the paper says." He turned to Wally. "Someday we'll learn—won't we?"

Wally nodded. *Sure. Someday.* Someday when the present literacy class "graduated" and we could start a new class with others who wanted to learn. Someday when he could take time off Bible story translation. Someday when he and Paul did not have to spend so much time on medical work, visitation, and teaching.

David rested his head wearily in his hands. "Wally, whatever will become of us? We're really ignorant. We'll never make it. I really thought for a while that we had become outsiders, but we're no different from the way we used to be. We still get angry. We don't know anything about friendliness at all. We're still Yanoamö, and I think we always will be."

"Of course you are," Wally agreed. "But why do you think that only you Yanoamö become discouraged? Do you think we outsiders never gossip or quarrel?" The startled faces that turned his way were answer enough. "We're just like you," he told them. "We're all prone to think the worst of people. We all lose our tempers."

After a moment of stunned silence, they broke into relieved laughter. Maybe they were normal after all. José shook Wally by the arm. "Brother," he grinned, shifting his controversial wad of tobacco leaves to the opposite side of his mouth. "Tell me something. Do you ever get angry at Margarita? Do you outsiders quarrel with your wives, too?"

Everyone leaned forward intently. They must have wondered why Paul and Wally were grinning at each other. Wally cleared his throat impressively. "Do I ever!" he exclaimed. "You should hear me! She *never* makes my coffee until I've asked her twice!"

The laughter subsided and Enrique spoke. "Wally, we won't quit following the Lord. Don't think you've spent all this time among us in vain."

"That's right," the others nodded. "We'll put away our anger and confess our sin to the Lord. He'll give us friendship with one another again."

"Sure He will," Wally encouraged them. "He can give you friendship with everybody—even your enemies. Don't be discouraged."

"Wally," Enrique interrupted, "I'm through criticizing Miguel's people. Who knows? Maybe they *are* sincere. Next time they come for a meeting, you call us and we'll come and sit with them. We'll find out for ourselves whether or not they're interested in following the Lord. Maybe we've been listening to too much gossip."

Miguel's eldest son, Carlos, was sitting in the meeting. He had close ties both with the people of the big savannah, where he lived with his wife, and with his parents' village on the opposite side of the savannah; and he had always felt frustrated over the lack of communication between the two groups. He had tried to convince each village of the good will of the other, but with little success. Too many people felt duty bound to keep the memory of past grievances alive, and an abundance of gossip fueled the fires of suspicion. At the close of the meeting, Carlos hurried to the roundhouse, untied his hammock, and told his wife he would be back in the morning.

Late that evening, while the welcome sound of prayer once more drifted to our house in the still night air, Carlos sat beside his parents' campfire on the other side of the savannah, coaxing them to bring the group to our house for an early morning meeting the following day.

Miguel's brother bounded into the porch and broke into a joyful dance as he pranced back and forth before the partition that separated him from the kitchen. His face was streaked liberally with purple dye, and the blue feathers dangling from his ears bounced in time to the rhythmic stomping of his feet. A fleeting grin flashed across his face as he caught our attention.

Then he settled into a stiff, formal stance with his bow and arrows held tightly to his chest. Swaying slightly, he began to chant an announcement that all his people were coming across the savannah to call for a meeting.

"Ay! That's the way!" Wally laughed in appreciation of his

The Long Road to Peace

originality. Not many meetings were proclaimed with such a flourish! Purple Face responded to the applause with a fresh burst of enthusiasm. With a loud hoot, he bounded across the porch and danced an energetic encore for a few moments more before he came to an exhausted halt and dropped to a bench beside Wally.

"How was that?" he panted.

"Very nice!" Wally laughed. "Is everyone really coming?"

The door opened as if in answer, and Miguel's people surged into the porch in happy confusion. "There! Didn't I tell you?" Purple Face exclaimed. "All of us! Even the old women!"

I leaned over the partition to watch the usual scramble for seats. The women sat on the floor in the doorway, where they could make a quick exit if their children demanded attention, and the men following behind were obliged to step over them, struggling for balance as they pushed one another inside. A loud ring of laughter filled the room as one of them suffered the embarrassment of stumbling into his mother-in-law. Quickly depositing their bows and arrows in a corner, the men scrambled in rowdy disarray for the empty seats on the opposite side of the porch.

The women began to clamor for me to join them. I usually enjoyed the close contact that such meetings demanded, but indoor meetings had problems all their own. Sitting among the women on poles in the yard allowed a certain amount of freedom, but nothing was more devastating than being hemmed into a corner on the floor by a crowd of mothers with bare-bottomed babies.

Miguel's wife jumped up to the partition to coax me with hugs to come to the meeting, but I had to refuse. Wally wanted to mimeograph some new booklets in the afternoon, and I was still working on the final stencils.

Paul and Marty arrived with the last stragglers and handed a stack of songbooks to one of the boys for distribution. Miguel's son, Carlos, set his bow and arrows aside and crouched in front of Wally. He smiled with justifiable pride. "I've brought them all!" he laughed softly. "Does Enrique know we're here?"

Wally nodded. One of the boys had already left for the village to announce their arrival. Carlos smiled and grasped Wally by the

Treasures of Darkness

arm. "Will they really come?" he grinned, studying Wally's eyes for assurance. "Do you think they'll really meet with us?"

"Of course," Wally answered, with more confidence than he actually felt. "They *said* they'd come, didn't they?"

Carlos nodded hesitantly and stretched to his feet.

Miguel stood up and looked out the window toward the roundhouse. Everyone watched him, waiting for an indication that the confrontation with Enrique's village was really going to take place. "Nobody's coming yet," he frowned.

Carlos fidgeted uneasily, and the old women muttered disgustedly that they *knew* they should not have bothered coming.

Suddenly Miguel's face broke into a smile. "Here they come!" he whispered excitedly, quickly resuming his seat by the fire and warming his hands over the flames. "They're coming with all their clothes on!" That might have been an odd thing to say anywhere else in the world, but to Miguel's people, who were excitedly shifting position to make a little more space on the benches, the startling variety of odds and ends that decorated the approaching delegation lent the occasion an unmistakable air of dignity.

The door swung open, and Enrique surveyed the crowded porch with pleased surprise. He nodded toward Miguel and stepped into the room with a smile. He was followed by ten or twelve others. "*All* of you came!" he murmured, setting his bow and arrows in the corner and joining Miguel.

"Of course," Miguel answered with a modest smile.

When the singing was over, Enrique announced that he was going to pray. He moved closer to Miguel and told everyone to bow their head. No time was wasted on preliminaries.

"Why is it," he asked the Lord, "that my friend here beside me doesn't like me? Why is it that he talks about me and says I don't really know You at all? Why does he tell his people not to listen to me?" On he prayed, listing his grievances to the Lord while my stomach tightened in a hard knot. What on earth was he trying to do? Start a riot?

Miguel said not a word. Neither he nor any of the others seemed the least disturbed by the proceedings. When Enrique finished,

Miguel shuffled into position facing Enrique, and cleared his throat. That was when we began to catch on.

We were witnessing a revision of the traditional method of settling prolonged disputes. In the same way they had formerly faced one another to chant formal accusations and rebuttals, they were facing one another now to speak their minds through a mutually trusted Intermediary.

Miguel warmed up by asking God to make them friends again, and then he began to comment on Enrique's prayer. "Why does my good friend think I lie about him? Who would tell him something like that? Why should I say anything against the one who helped me to find You? Doesn't he teach my own son to pray? Isn't he the one who asks that You fill my son with Your Spirit? Who is it that tells lies? Who is it that carries gossip back and forth?"

Enrique interjected exclamations of agreement every so often, slapping himself on the thigh for extra emphasis to declare publicly his unity with Miguel. Then around the circle, the others thanked the Lord that He was able to dispel their anger.

The meeting adjourned, and both groups mingled happily together while Miguel's people presented us with money they had saved from the sale of bananas we had purchased earlier. They wanted to buy booklets for a trip to the Shamatali area, and before they left, José and his brothers had decided to accompany them. A new friendship with their neighbors from the other side of the savannah had now been initiated, and the time had come to try to put brotherly love into action a little farther from home.

It seemed that we were finally witnessing a solid foundation for the precarious world of interrelationships, and though we realized it would take time and trials to establish a permanent affinity between people who had traditionally viewed one another with suspicion, we were happy with the progress we saw.

Both Miguel's village and José's people began making frequent trips to share the Gospel in Shamatali territory, and their enthusiasm grew as they saw the Word take root in the hearts of a few of their kinsmen there.

The newness of life on the big savannah stirred a desire in

Timoteo's heart, too, and his role of village defender lost its appeal. He was suddenly weary of warfare and of the constant tension it involved. His arrows had killed three men already, but his fame could not provide the satisfaction he sought. He followed the men to the porch one evening and bowed his heart before the Lord.

"I'm through," he said. "I always wanted to be fearless and brave, but now I just want a heart that's peaceful. *You* can be our defense. You're the One who's been protecting us. No one but You could have kept back the raiders for this long."

He rehearsed his history before the Lord and thanked Him for preventing the plans he had made to kill some of us outsiders. I shuddered involuntarily, recalling the fears I had fought during our first months on the big savannah. There really had been plans to harm us.

"They really made me angry," he prayed. "But You stopped me from killing them. What would have happened to us if I'd shot them? Our only hope would have vanished with them."

While Samuel continued his attempts at reaching a peaceful settlement with the enemy village, the people of the big savannah tried to restore friendly relationships in other areas where contact had long ago been severed with many distant villages.

It was a discouraging proposition because of the suspicion that overtures of friendship were only a trick to catch the unsuspecting off guard, but a group of people from beyond the western range of mountains finally accepted their invitation to come and see for themselves that things were different on the big savannah.

The shouts and screams that erupted when the people from the west filed into the village froze us with momentary terror. Even the villagers sitting with us were not sure for a moment that the sounds were happy. Then they jumped to their feet. "It's the sound of a welcome!" they shouted excitedly, grabbing their bows and arrows. "And it must be people who haven't been here for a long, long time!"

Soon, Enrique's sister, Doré burst in with the breathless announcement that distant relatives had arrived. Long ago, during a struggle with José's family and Miguel's group, they had fled for safety to the other side of the mountains. A few people uninvolved in the initial conflict had visited them once in a while to share the Gospel, but they had never before ventured back to the area from which Miguel and José had driven them.

Neither had they ever seen anyone from the outside world. Doré had been dispatched to take the Sadles and us to the village as "Exhibit A." We followed her to the roundhouse, and after making a futile attempt to converse with the women, we joined the men in David's house. All the visitors were resplendent in red and black paint, brilliant feathers, and white beads. Two of them stood before the assembled men in a ritual designed to make their trip worth the effort.

"Who's going to give?" chanted one, bending and twisting his body in rhythmic accentuation of his request. "Who's going to give to me? Give to me? Who's going to give me an ax? An ax?"

"An ax? Yes, an ax." José responded, in an answering chant that encouraged the visitor to continue.

"Where do I get an ax? How can I garden without an ax? Without an ax?"

"How can he garden without an ax?" José echoed, swaying back and forth as he relayed the request to the others around him.

"The people to the south have axes," the visitor continued. "And people to the east have axes. Where will we get our axes?"

The ceremony was loud and colorful as the two visitors kept up a simultaneous chant with different sections of the surrounding crowd. Fortunately, a new shipment of trade goods was in circulation. All the while the chant continued, the eager hosts presented the items requested, and vied with one another for the privilege of being able to place something of value at the feet of the visitors.

Roman Nose jumped to his feet when the visitor before him began to chant a request for a knife. "I've got one!" he whispered to José. "I just bought one from Paul yesterday."

He ran to his shelter to find his trophy, but José knocked him over in his enthusiasm to overtake him. "No, no! I'll give him mine!" he insisted. "You give the red material you bought for a loincloth!" There was a mad scramble in every direction, and the excitement of giving seemed more than that of receiving. David's father sauntered in with a wide grin, holding a flashlight behind his back in readiness for the time someone would ask for one.

Enrique had planned on bringing the visitors to our house for a late afternoon meeting, but as the time approached he changed his mind. He decided they were too frightened of us to profit from such an experience and supposed that he could present the Gospel more clearly than we could anyway. So he came to the house to borrow some booklets and called the people together in the village.

The visit might have been termed a total success had it not been for an impulsive act by Miguel's village. Someone hurried across the savannah to let Miguel know that the people from beyond the western ridge had arrived, and he was indignant. He and his brothers had prided themselves on winning the feud that had chased those people to the other side of the mountains, and they lacked the graciousness to accept their visit as anything more than a defiant insult to their victory. They stalked angrily into Enrique's village at dusk, and chanted old grievances throughout the night. They drew the visitors into a verbal battle that undid everyone's efforts at trying to restore peace.

Early the following morning, the visitors packed up angrily and left for home, convinced that the people of the big savannah had not changed much after all. They were miles away by the time Miguel's people came to their senses and recognized the damage they had caused. It was too late to correct the harm done, but it was a lesson that stayed painfully fresh in everyone's mind for a long time. They were soon going to have another chance to prove their hospitality.

The afternoon meeting had just come to a close, and the men were still gathered around Paul, staring in fascination at the new illustrations of Daniel in the lion's den, when Samuel arrived from the Balafili valley. He had come to let us know that the little shack they had been preparing for us had now been completed and the villages in his area were awaiting our long overdue visit.

The Long Road to Peace

He left the following morning, assured that we would be flying over to the tiny strip near his home in four more days. We began feverish preparations for a ten-day stay with the people of the Balafili valley.

A crowd gathered around the plane on the day of our departure from the big savannah and promised to pray for us as we sought a friendly relationship with the many groups who still sympathized with the enemy village. They faded in a blur as we sped down the runway in the little Cessna and lifted into the air. In a turmoil of rough currents we bounced over the mountains, and a few moments later we were circling the neighboring valley.

Wally began to point out the scattering of villages that dotted the jungles and the grasslands. On a distant hillside was the enemy village, and not far away, thin columns of pale smoke rose from two settlements with whom they were closely allied. Below us on a small savannah was another cluster of villages whose affiliation with the enemy group was not so strong. Samuel's village was one of them, and it was unique in its friendship with the people of the big savannah.

We rolled to a stop on the grassy strip, and with customary enthusiasm, the Yanoamö surrounded the plane and helped carry our supplies to the little hut they had erected nearby. Wally was well known among them, since he and Paul often visited the area, but most of them had never seen the children and me, and we caused quite a sensation. A perpetual crowd surrounded us to study our methods of eating, sleeping, talking, laughing, and bathing.

Samuel was overjoyed that we had finally come as a family to spend a few days among the people of his valley, and took upon himself the task of arranging regular afternoon meetings. Representatives of five surrounding villages flocked to the house day by day, and Samuel's friends and relatives mingled with the crowds to add their own explanations to the concentration of teaching.

Many were hindered in a wholehearted commitment to the Lord by their unwillingness to relinquish old animosities. Their ties with the enemy village were well established, and though they had never participated in the warfare, they had a consuming passion to see vengeance taken against the people of the big savannah. They had little desire to lose their anger, and they scoffed at the possibility that the men of the big savannah had undergone a change of heart.

The leaders often gathered by our house in the cool of the evening to discuss the warfare. The days passed, and the initial skepticism vanished. Many began to question us concerning the fact that the people of the big savannah were said to be peaceable now. Men whose hearts had hardened over the years gave way to sentimental memories and asked us concerning individuals with whom they had once been friendly.

A witchdoctor of the village where Wally had tried unsuccessfully to save the life of the woman who had been bitten by a snake became a regular participant in the evening discussions. The bitterness in his heart began to fade as the week progressed, and an occasional loneliness crept into his voice as he recalled happier times.

"I'd promised my daughter to Pedro," he remembered. "And she'd already moved over there. We were happy then."

"Pedro used to come and visit me. He'd tell people how much he missed his dear old father-in-law." He paused in private reflection, and the softness in his voice disappeared as he continued. "But that was before they started shooting my friends. I ran right over and took her back. I've given her to Pedro's enemies."

He came to a meeting a day or so later, with his face painted bright red. He squatted on the ground, uneasily shifting his weight as the men around him prayed. Then he cleared his throat and shuffled into position beside Samuel. His day had arrived.

I thrilled at the words of his prayer as he asked the Lord in wonderment how such fierce anger as his could have disappeared. *Lord,* I prayed, *if only this would spread! If only You'd reach over the mountains now and touch the enemy village!*

Encouraged by the fact that many of the enemy village sympathizers now felt the first longings for a peaceful way of life, Wally and Samuel decided to travel over the hills to the enemy

The Long Road to Peace

village once again, in an attempt to dissuade them from carrying the fight any further. But they returned with the discouraging report that they had found the village evacuated. It was three days later that we found out the reason for the empty village, and our disappointment changed to excitement.

The Balafili women that had been seated with me in the doorway of our little shack scrambled to their feet and grabbed their baskets in a flurry of squeals and giggles. One of them stopped long enough to whisper a hasty explanation. "Men from a different village are coming!" she laughed, pointing toward the airstrip with her chin. "We have to leave, or people will talk about us!"

Wally and five young men who were engaged in animated conversation were coming up the path from the runway. Happy shouts of laughter rang out as they approached, and when Wally sat down on a log by the campfire, they crowded around enthusiastically to share the news from home. Everyone was in good health. The village had been rebuilt. There was plenty of meat.

"Who are they?" I whispered to Wally as they busied themselves around the campfire. "Did we see their village from the air?"

"Friends of mine," he smiled. "Nice guys, aren't they?"

"Very nice," I agreed. "Where are they from?"

He paused a moment, unwilling to spoil my impression. He studied the faces of his newly arrived friends seated around the fire roasting plantains. "From the enemy village."

I should not have been shocked. We were, after all, in the Balafili valley–in enemy territory. I stared at them in fascination. They came nowhere near the mental image I had of terrorist raiders. Our anonymous adversaries were suddenly elevated to the level of personal friends, and peace seemed so very urgent.

One of them leaned forward and whispered something to Wally. "Really?" Wally exclaimed in startled surprise.

"That's right! That's right!" they laughed, all talking at once as they crowded around to confirm their announcement. "We're through! We're not going to shoot anymore! We're scared of hellfire!"

Their theology may have been a little fuzzy, but it did not seem the opportune time to debate the issue. "We've rebuilt the roundhouse," they continued with happy excitement. "That's why you and Samuel couldn't find us! We're living closer now! Right over that mountain. Would we relocate in this area if we still intended to fight? Would we move our village closer to the big savannah?"

We struggled to keep our excitement under control, hardly daring to believe that their report was true. We knew that the people of the big savannah would accept such news cautiously. Only time could prove the reliability of such announcements.

We had been with the Balafili people for a week and a half when we finally made plans to head back over the mountains to the big savannah. Samuel volunteered as a guide for the return trip, and Wally told him he could hire two more men to help carry Janice and Davey, our two youngest children, in case they tired on the trail. Samuel deliberately chose two men from one of the villages who had sympathized with the enemy group.

Their acceptance was uneasy, and so were our assurances that all would be well. Who could tell what might happen in a sudden, emotional confrontation?

We locked our belonging in a steel drum, bid a tearful farewell to the crowd that had gathered to bewail our departure, and promised to return as soon as possible.

Eight long hours later, we arrived on the big savannah. The two jittery guides followed Samuel and us into the house to await whatever fate would befall them. Samuel would have gone on to the roundhouse by himself had he been alone, but he was hesitant to usher the other two into the village unannounced. Nor did he want to leave them alone in the porch, since he felt responsible for their welfare.

We sent a message to Enrique via one of the children playing on the airstrip telling him how we had promised our guides a friendly reception. The rest was up to them.

Word came back that Samuel was to conduct them to Octavio's

The Long Road to Peace

shelter for the night.

Their entrance to the village lacked the usual color, since they had been too nervous to make an official entrance as visitors, but they passed the night uneventfully. The following morning they returned to our house to show us the gifts they had received from their hosts, and then they left once more for the Balafili valley.

Their safe return to their own village was heralded as a breakthrough in relationships between the two groups, and a few others who had been loosely affiliated with the enemy village began making cautious visits to the big savannah as well. But even so, none of us were prepared for what the Lord was doing.

It was two days before Christmas. A large group of us was standing in front of the Shadles' house when someone noticed a long line of people approaching from the south end of the savannah.

"*Uno, dos, tres–*" one of the boys began, practicing the Spanish numbers we had been teaching as he counted the long line of people moving toward us.

"It's visitors! More visitors!" David shouted excitedly. "Look at their decorations!"

The women scrambled for their children and their baskets, and the men quickly gathered their bows and arrows. Then they all rushed down the path to the roundhouse. Everyone wanted to be seated in his hammock so they would all be ready to jump up and join their voices in a rousing welcome when the visitors made their entrance.

David's brother was one of the last to leave. He lingered beside us with a few children who were not too concerned with protocol, and he strained to recognize the visitors briskly approaching the end of the airstrip. He concluded they must be from Samuel's village and was just about to run after the others already nearing the roundhouse when a little girl jerked me by the arm.

"Margarita!" she gasped. "That man–that man in the middle– the thin one! He is from the enemy village! I've seen him at Samuel's house when I stayed with my father over there!"

I stared at her in stunned amazement, and David's brother

Treasures of Darkness

stooped to ask her what she had said. He did not think he had heard correctly. But she would not repeat it.

"I'm scared," she whispered, squeezing my hand and inching closer.

He squinted once more toward the airstrip and studied the long line of visitors hurrying toward us. "She can't see that far," he scoffed. "And nobody from the enemy village would walk right in among us." He paused for a moment, searching our faces for an opinion he could quote at the village, and then he ran after the others.

We moved to the edge of the runway with Paul and Marty, hardly daring to consider the possibility that the little girl might be right, but too excited to ignore it altogether. Custom had it that visitors nearing their destination were not to be interrupted on their way to the village, and the grim procession nearing us did nothing to encourage any infraction of the rule. The dark colors with which they had been painted reflected a certain intensity of purpose, and though many of them knew us well, they filed past with eyes straight ahead, like soldiers on parade.

Two men from Samuel's village were in the lead, and behind them was the Balafili witchdoctor who had so recently marveled that the Lord had been able to dispel his anger. Two more from Samuel's village followed, and then an old man I did not recognize.

Wally and Paul began an excited exchange. "She's right!" I could hear them whispering beside me. "It's the old captain of the enemy village!" My throat was tight. The tension they felt as they neared their destination must have been contagious. The little girl's fingers tightened around my clammy hand.

"That's him," she whispered in a voice barely audible. I squeezed her hand in answer and studied the old man passing by. His build was slight, his head held high, and I tried in vain to imagine the emotion hidden behind his stoic expression as he strode toward the roundhouse he considered his enemy village. Whatever misgivings he had suffered were left behind when they marched on to the big savannah and made their decision irreversible.

Samuel followed him, grimly intent on the confrontation so

The Long Road to Peace

close before them. He had worked toward it for a long time, and he was well aware of his awesome responsibility in escorting the old man before him into the midst of his enemies. Anything could happen. He knew that many well-intentioned truces had erupted in violence at just such a climatic confrontation. His brothers stepped quickly behind him, and two women brought up the rear.

Shoulders squared for action, they passed us quickly and disappeared from sight as they followed the trail down to the swamp that separated us from the village. We moved back from the runway and waited for them to appear on the opposite side of the swamp.

One by one they came into view and hurried the final hundred paces to the roundhouse. We followed them with our eyes to the edge of the village and held our breath as they disappeared inside.

Lord, don't let anything go wrong now.

We waited for what seemed an eternity, wondering how the men would react when they realized whom Samuel had brought; wondering how José and Timoteo would stand the test; wondering if the visitors would be offered the same grudging hospitality that had been given the two guides who had returned with us from the Balafili valley.

Then a tremendous shout of welcome rang out and filled the earth and heaven with rejoicing. The tumult of their reception lasted a full sixty seconds. We laughed! We cheered! We clapped our hands and danced for joy and shouted "Merry Christmas" to one another!

Half an hour later, one of José's younger brothers ran excitedly past the house only to return a few moments later with a breathless request for a machete. José had sent him to the garden to cut down some plantains for the visitors. Giddy with the excitement of the afternoon, he had forgotten to take his machete. And equally immune to the mundane cares of the regular routine, we cheerfully handed over one of ours without a complaint!

So far we had purposely avoided involvement to allow them flexibility in working out the details of their meeting, but we could hardly contain our curiosity any longer. Paul decided to run down to the village and see what was happening.

Everything was quiet when he arrived. He wandered into Enrique's house, thinking that would be the obvious place to find the old man from the enemy village; but a quick glance around the room proved his supposition wrong. The visitors who had been invited into Enrique's home were both from Samuel's village.

Realizing that Paul had arrived with the express purpose of welcoming the old man to the big savannah, Enrique decided to accompany him to the opposite side of the village, where he was being hosted. Enrique had not yet spoken with the old man either.

They crossed the village clearing, and when the others realized whom they were looking for, they directed them to José's shelter. José, of all people! Paul and Enrique ducked under the leaves into José's home and made their way to the hammock where the old man was resting. José smiled a wide welcome, left his hearth, and joined them in conversation with the guest of honor.

Night fell, and they organized a marathon prayer meeting at David's house, to which they invited all the visitors. José came down early the following morning to fill us in on the details.

"We didn't chant with them!" he grinned. "We just prayed. Not one person spoke in anger! Not even me!" He chuckled at the memory of it. No one could have been more amazed at the change in José than José himself. "The old man told us his people want to know the Lord. He says they don't want to fight any more." He paused and thought it over. "Who knows?" he mused. "Maybe it's true!"

Our attention was diverted by a commotion outside, as yesterday's tense visitors cheerfully gathered around Paul and Marty to bid them farewell. They were on their way back to the Balafili valley, anxious to assure the fearful ones who had stayed behind that they had been peacefully received on the big savannah. The war was over.

8

Tempted and Tried

The trying of your faith worketh patience.

James 1:3

Jaime squatted over the bundle of meat he had just unwrapped, and deftly whacked the shells from two small armadillos. He divided his catch between Marty and me, then borrowed Paul's file to put a new edge on his machete. He was from Samuel's village. He was the same man who had enjoyed the party at our fireside when Jill and I had attempted to win the friendship of his two wives. We gathered around him to hear the latest Balafili news.

"Did you know Wishiquimi is hurt?" he asked, without a pause in his work.

"No."

"Her leg's been cut off," he said, testing the edge of his blade against his thumb. "She kept running around, and her husband finally got angry. He's through with her. That's it."

We looked at one another, a little startled, wondering at the accuracy of his report. Wishiquimi's reputation left considerable room for improvement, and she would not have been the first girl to receive a violent divorce for infidelity, but someone would surely have reported a medical emergency so extreme. She had married into Samuel's village, but all her relatives lived beside us in the roundhouse on the big savannah. Someone would *surely* have let *them* know at least.

"She's getting a little better now?" Wally suggested.

"No, of course not," Jaime answered impatiently. "She's ruined. Her foot dangles. How can she get better?"

"But no one came for me," Wally persisted. "Someone would have told us."

"Who knows what they would do?" Jaime shrugged. "I didn't stay around. We were leaving the next morning on a hunt."

He was not interested in continuing the conversation. He stretched to his feet, handed Paul the file, and prepared to leave.

We did not know what to do. We hesitated to share the news Jaime had brought, because we had no way of knowing how factual it was. And we dreaded the possible reaction. Wishiquimi's husband may have been the guilty party, but his entire village would be held responsible if the girl was really damaged. The thought that the people on the big savannah could suddenly be plunged into warfare with Samuel's village was staggering. *Lord,* I prayed, *Yanoamö peace is such a fragile thing!*

Wally confided in Enrique and a few others soon to be leaving on a missionary trip to the north. They shrugged their shoulders and supposed that someone would have reported to Wishiquimi's relatives if the story were really true. We tried to believe it was a typical exaggeration, but when little Juancito smashed his foot a few days later and a doctor had to be flown in to repair the damage, Wally decided to make use of the plane's availability to check on Wishiquimi's condition.

Juancito was carried into our front room and stretched out on a long table. While Paul and Marty helped the doctor do the necessary work on his foot, Jim Hurd flew Wally over to the Balafili valley, where they landed on the runway near Samuel's village.

Operations in the front room were just about finished when the plane returned, and Wally jumped out with the grim announcement that the girl's condition had been every bit as bad as Jaime's report had indicated.

Wally and Jim Hurd had hiked from the runway to Samuel's village, accompanied by a small group of women who had met the plane. Wally could tell by their attitudes that Wishiquimi was in serious condition. The women seemed frightened with the possibility that Wally might want to retaliate. "What will you do if her husband gets angry over your interference?" they asked nervously. "What will you do if he tells you to go away and leave her alone?"

"He won't," Wally assured them, annoyed with the possibility.

They found Wishiquimi in a hastily constructed shack behind the village, where she had been moved to spare the others her constant groans and the stench of rotting flesh. Piecing the story together, they judged that the damage had been done nine days earlier, the same day the captain of the enemy village had arrived on the big savannah and we had rejoiced to see the end of the war.

"That very day?" I asked, interrupting the account. Wally nodded. *Typical*, I thought, suddenly overwhelmed with a heavy weariness. *Every advance contested.* Wally continued the story, and I listened numbly.

During those nine days of suffering, Wishiquimi had lain unattended in her filthy hammock, caked with blood and dirt. Flies and gnats swarmed around her festering leg, and jagged bone protruded from the wide, putrid gash that almost severed her leg below the knee.

Her husband was not home when Wally and Jim arrived on the scene. He had left the village angrily–angry that his wife's unfaithfulness had provoked him to such violence.

The women quickly untied Wishiquimi's hammock, and transported her slowly to the airstrip. Every movement of the hammock was torture to her as she swung between the two women carrying her along the trail, and an old matriarch walking beside her held her leg above and below the wound in an attempt to prevent her dangling foot from swaying the wrong direction.

She was loaded into the plane, and the women watched soberly as Wally secured her in place for the flight back to the big savannah, where her relatives anxiously awaited her arrival.

We went out to the plane to bring her into the house. Wishiquimi's family crowded around to examine her condition, and as the men realized the extent of the damage, they turned their backs one by one and walked away. Their background gave them

Treasures of Darkness

no reason to hope for her recovery, and the longer they looked at her, the angrier they became. The sight of her misery stirred a rage they were struggling to control.

"Wally," David stammered, "I thought I'd never want to shoot another man. I thought my anger had gone forever. But if something happens to her—if she doesn't recover..." He could not finish the sentence. He turned and walked away.

Jim Hurd and Wally carried her in from the plane, and since Juancito still occupied the long table in the front room, they stretched her out on the kitchen table on an old blanket. She was sobbing miserably, and everything we did to try to alleviate the pain seemed to add to her discomfort. The women of the village crowded around her and wept in frustration.

The doctor eyed her from a distance while he finished a cup of coffee. It was not necessary to move closer to appraise her condition. The smell of rotting flesh filled the room.

After a few moments, we shooed the visitors from Wishiquimi's side, and the doctor moved forward for a quick examination. "It will have to come off," he stated matter-of-factly. "There's not enough holding it together, and it is already cold below the knee." He studied her face for a moment, and she watched him with frightened eyes. Then he moved away to where the air was fresher. "We'll have to amputate above the knee," he said. "And in her condition, who knows whether she'll live through it?"

The doctor began collecting his equipment, and we promised to pass on a radio message later in the day to let him know whether or not Wishiquimi's family would give permission for her to fly out to a hospital for amputation.

By late afternoon the initial shock had worn off, and we were able to meet with her relatives and carry on a reasonable discussion of her chances of recovery. They sat around us silently listening to the cold, hard words the doctor had spoken, nodding reluctant agreement that it had to be done. "They'll save as much as they can," Wally assured them. "But once she's flown out there it will all be up to the doctors. You won't be able to change your minds. If you're nervous about sending her, you can keep her here."

"But you can't put her leg back together?"

"No."

"OK," they said. "Call the plane. We'll send her out in the morning."

Paul and Marty Shadle agreed to accompany her to civilization to soften the cultural transition and to speak for her to the medical staff, who understood no Yanoamö.

Early the following morning, while Wally was helping the Shadles with hurried preparations for their unexpected departure, I went down to the village to see how Wishiquimi had passed the night. She was propped in a sitting position and eating a roasted plantain. She grinned a welcome as I approached, and it was difficult to realize that she was the same person for whom we had despaired the day before. Just being back with her own people had given her new optimism.

Her relatives gathered around to ask if the plane was on its way and to discuss the coming operation. I tried to make amputations sound routine, then changed the subject and told them I had sewed two new dresses for her the night before. They nodded their approval and accepted it as her due compensation, though my reasons had been a little more practical. Nakedness may have been a way of life for *them*, but we did not want to subject her to the curious, amused gaze of the outside world by sending her off bundled in one lonely G-string. In spite of the fact that many of the Yanoamö now owned some sort of covering, they preferred to save their clothing for special occasions. They made no connection between wearing apparel and modesty. Clothing was strictly ornamental.

"They're going to ask what your name is, too," I laughed. "People in the doctor's house always do that! They write everyone's name on paper." They exchanged dismayed glances, and her mother shook me by the arm.

"Little One," she whispered. "Give her a name right now. Tell her what to say." I hesitated a moment, and she snorted her annoyance, pulling away from me and jerking her head angrily.

Treasures of Darkness

"Why is it that you outsiders always give names to everyone else, and never name us?" she demanded.

"Because you never ask for Spanish names," I retorted, imitating her indignation. She smiled reluctantly and shifted closer against me on our common piece of firewood. She put an arm around my shoulders apologetically.

"All right," she smiled. "Just give her a name right now."

I paused in thought for a moment or two, and they waited with respectful silence for the inspiration they hoped would suggest a name to my mind. "Sofia!" I said. "Her name can be Sofia!" It was a name that no one else of their acquaintance had, and it was easily pronounced by a Yanoamö tongue. Those were the two basic requirements. "Just tell them your name is Sofia Parima!"

They smiled their appreciation, and whispered her new name under their breath.

An hour later they brought her to the house for a bath and a meal before the plane arrived. The room was crowded with mournful visitors who examined her condition and responded with tears or anger. I carried out a pail of warm water, some soap and wash cloths, and tried to prepare Wishiquimi for entrance to the outside world.

She winced as I dabbed at the blood caked to her broken leg, and I soon decided to leave it for the nurses, and concentrate on the rest of her. No amount of scrubbing seemed to make a dent on the accumulation of dirt, dust, and vegetable dye that had been ground into her skin for twenty years or so. Occasional soapless bathing in a cold stream had not really seemed to accomplish very much for her. Finally, I rummaged through a kitchen cupboard and came up with a cleanser marketed for stubborn stains on pots and pans. Miraculous! It would have made a fantastic commercial!

The women gathered around us in a wide-eyed circle, stunned by the fact that Wishiquimi's natural color was so many shades lighter than they had expected. "Margarita!" they exclaimed with excited laughter. "She looks just like you! She's not one of us at all! She's an outsider!" The patient was equally delighted with her new complexion and proud of the admiring smiles that came her way.

Tempted and Tried

We helped her into one of her new dresses and showed her where her new name was printed on it for identification. "And here's a comb," I said, offering her a few items Marty and I had decided to donate to the cause. "And a mirror, and your other dress, and some books to look at."

She smiled her thanks and stacked her treasures on the bench beside her. "And here's a bag for you to keep everything in," I said, holding forth a faded pillowcase boldly lettered with the name 'Sofia Parima' on both sides.

The sound of the plane's engine disrupted the cheerfulness of the scene, and the women began to wail. Before long Wishiquimi was being lifted once more into the aircraft, and Paul and Marty were climbing in beside her. A prayer was offered for her safe return, and she set off on the longest journey of her life.

The crowd dispersed, and Wally and I turned wearily back to the house, relieved to have passed medical responsibility for Wishiquimi into more competent hands. But the problems engendered by her injury were only beginning.

For a while following Wishiquimi's bloody divorce, the people of Samuel's village kept prudently out of sight. The severity of the blame laid upon them would be proportionate to the girl's final condition. The word was received from the Shadles that amputation might not be necessary, and the Balafili people breathed a sigh of relief. In a cautious attempt to test the durability of their friendship, Samuel sent Jaime over to the big savannah to see if there was any talk of retaliation.

Jaime arrived with a gift of roasted caterpillars for his in-laws, and discovered that the younger of his two wives had run away. Her parents, into whose keeping he had entrusted her for a few weeks, had done nothing to stop her. No explanation was necessary. Jaime knew that their refusal to protect his interests was an obvious protest against the damage done Wishiquimi.

Quite a few families had spread out into the jungles to camp in scattered shelters near newly developed garden plots, and Jaime's wife was with them. To be more specific, she was hiding at a campsite high on a hill overlooking the big savannah, and she was trying to talk Pedro into taking her as his wife.

Jaime crept to Pedro's camp in the dark of night, but word of his coming preceded him. He burst into camp to find the hammock next to Pedro's empty. His child-wife had already fled to the safety of the surrounding jungles.

"Where is she?" Jaime demanded.

"She's gone!" came a chorus of answers from nearby shelters. "She's afraid of you wild men of Balafili!"

Jaime knew he was trapped. Panicked with the realization that he had to reap another man's sins, he shouted angrily into the darkness, "Why should she fear *me*? When have *I* ever sent her home with scars?" But his arguments were pointless. Specific guilt was not that important. He was part of the village that had injured Wishiquimi, and that was all that mattered.

Pedro felt a little uneasy. He *liked* Jaime. But the prospects of an easily arranged marriage sounded irresistible. "I never *tried* to steal her away," he finally muttered. "It was *her* idea."

Jaime stormed out of camp and made his way to our house, where he got us out of bed to let us know what had transpired. His frustration was overwhelming. His voice trembled and his arms shook. "Brother," he said, leaning forward to watch the expression on Wally's face in the flickering lamplight. "They told me you said it is all right for Pedro to take her. They say you told him nobody should have two wives anyway."

"That's not true," Wally answered. "I haven't even *seen* Pedro since this happened. I always tell them God says one wife is best, but I would never suggest that anyone take another man's wife. That would be adultery. I tell them to keep the wives they already have. God warns against divorces." He paused a moment, scanning his memory for anything Pedro might use to vindicate his position. About half the men had more than one wife, and the subject often came up for discussion. "But I did say that husbands were free to give back second wives not yet come of age," he remembered. Jaime nodded and shuffled closer. "After all," Wally reasoned, "when they're that young you husbands have never really taken them anyway."

It took a moment for Jaime to realize that Wally was referring to a physical relationship. "What's *that* got to do with it?" he exploded. "Sex! Is that all you outsiders ever think of?"

Wally and I looked at one another with dismay. Who would have supposed *they* would consider *us* perverted?

"I've had her in my home since she was a little girl," Jaime continued with exasperation. "I've fed her. I've raised her." He leaned forward and drew a deep, calming breath. "Don't say she isn't mine," he pleaded. "I *like* her! All my relatives are going to cry when they hear she's been taken from me. We've swung our hammock around the campfire and laughed together! She's roasted my food and chopped my firewood! How can anyone say she isn't mine?"

"I don't say that," Wally assured him. "I just say men can give back child-wives if they *want* to. I'd never say she's not yours if you still claim her."

"Really?"

"Really."

Jaime got to his feet and moved toward the door, hesitating a moment to ask one final question. "Brother, you *will* tell them to give her back, won't you? Tell them we don't want to fight about it."

Wally nodded slowly. He could remind them what God's Word taught, but he could not guarantee the results. "And pray for me," Jaime added. "I'm really upset. My heart's in a turmoil."

Our hearts were in turmoil, too. We suspected that the group hiding the girl on the hillside would have *welcomed* outside interference. It would not have been the first time a few reckless individuals had rushed headlong into questionable schemes, trusting that more sane voices would call a halt to their actions. But *we* did not want to assume village leadership. Enrique and the others had not yet returned from their trip, so we tried to pass on the responsibility to the families still living in the roundhouse. But they had neither the experience nor the inclination to direct the affairs of others. They were content to pursue their own private interests and hope that Enrique would return to set things in order before any serious difficulty developed.

Pedro's family had been delighted with the prospects of a daughter-in-law, and Wishiquimi's people found Jaime's frustration deeply gratifying. There was a certain satisfaction in knowing they had been able to avenge their grief. But they lacked the support of the village to launch a serious attempt at withholding the girl from her rightful husband. The only interest they could seem to generate was among a few people whose passion for excitement always managed to obscure the generally accepted guidelines. For them, the challenge of hiding a runaway wife was exhilarating. They enjoyed the tension and reveled in the excitement of surprise visits from Jaime, as he made frequent trips from the Balafili valley to try to capture his renegade spouse.

Each unsuccessful effort added to Jaime's determination, and with each succeeding venture, more and more irate friends and relatives joined him in his search.

Pedro did not like to be the cause of such trouble. The girl's insistence on staying with him was flattering, but he did not really feel justified. Finally he came to the house to ask our advice, and relieved to find someone who would counsel him against the idea, he moved back to the village by himself. His family reluctantly followed, and Jaime's little wife was left on the hillside in the hands of a disorderly band of protectors.

Jungle camp-outs had a poor reputation of long standing, and no one seemed surprised when hints of immorality drifted back to the village. But when a report of rape and incest arrived, involving some who had professed to know the Lord, even the most complacent were shaken into action. They could not wait for Enrique to return. The commotion of the hillside was getting out of hand.

The suppressed emotion of days of frustration burst forth in a bedlam of angry accusations so effective that the campers moved sheepishly back to the village. The charges were all denied, and a simmering resentment settled over the village like an ominous storm cloud. Only two girls remained in the woods: Jaime's wife, timidly awaiting inevitable capture, and her companion, a young

Tempted and Tried

girl who was too ashamed to return to her home now that everyone knew of the humiliation she had suffered at the hands of her uncle Waldo and three other men.

Everyone bewailed Enrique's absence. He never would have allowed things to get so far out of control. But their dependence on him had been doing them more harm than good. He had become their conscience. We prepared ourselves to ride out the storm, and we trusted the Lord to teach the lessons the people needed to learn.

Jaime received a message that Pedro had relinquished all interest in the girl, and he hurried back to the savannah with a delegation of wife hunters determined to capture their prey. The mission was successful, but before we had time to breathe a sigh of relief, another problem developed.

The women's afternoon meeting had just come to a close, and I was heading wearily for the house. Most of the women had already gone around to the dispensary to ask Wally for a dab of Merthiolate or a spoon of cough syrup, when two men from the village rushed up to ask if Catalina had met with us. I had not heard her name mentioned in any scandals since her infatuation with Antonio had caused friction between Enrique and Timoteo, but something was obviously amiss. When the women told them she had not been at the meeting, they decided she must have run away. They hollered toward the village, and a group of men who had been waiting for the signal poured forth with all their weapons.

Some raced down the airstrip, and others cut through the savannah and disappeared into the jungle. All the angry men of the village had found a vent for their frustrations. They dashed past us into the woods, and in spite of my annoyance with Catalina, I hoped she was far away or well hidden.

A voice whispered that Enrique was back. We turned and saw him standing behind us, worn and haggard from the long trip over the mountains. Wally tried to smile a friendly welcome, but it was impossible to ignore the confusion of men screaming, women crying, and people running helter skelter. He nodded an acknowledgement, and seated himself dejectedly on a log. His enthusiasm to share the results of his efforts was lost in the pandemonium.

His friends crowded around him and brought him up to date with vivid accounts of Wishiquimi's injury, of the struggle over Jaime's wife, and of rape and incest. It was quite a welcome. It seemed that all the traditional violence and passion of the big savannah had broken loose around us, and I suddenly realized why Enrique occasionally succumbed to discouragement. The uproar caused by a few families was completely overwhelming the entire village.

Half an hour later, the men, grumbling that Catalina could not be found, began to trickle back to the village. She appeared the following morning and announced that she had lost her way in the jungles and been forced to spend the night in the woods. No one believed her, but by then they were too ashamed of themselves to renew the furor of the day before. Someone had made the appropriate observation that they had almost been in the same position as the Pharisees who took the adulterous woman to Jesus for punishment. They contented themselves by muttering threats of what would happen if she ever attempted to run away again.

Timoteo swung angrily in his hammock, thoroughly incensed that his niece should once again have come into public notoriety. The whole affair disgusted him completely–the anger, the immorality, the injustice of the past few weeks. And Catalina had almost suffered the penalty of it all. She had almost taken the brunt of everyone's anger.

He'd had enough! He launched into a tirade against the whole village, adding an extra dash of emphasis by claiming that even Wally and I despaired of ever seeing faithful believers on the big savannah. We heard of it a while later when Catalina came to the house with a group of women, demanding to know why we had been denouncing them all as hopeless, immoral liars.

They realized we were baffled by their accusations, and timidly acknowledged their source of information. Wally sent a message to the village asking if Timoteo would come to the house, and the boy who delivered the request added to the excitement by telling Timoteo that Wally had been calling him a liar. In Timoteo's frame of mind, those were fighting words.

He strode angrily down the path from the village, swinging his machete at his side. He came to a determined stop in front of the house, planted his feet firmly apart, and grasped his machete tightly to his chest. He began to sway back and forth.

"Outsider!" he screamed, spitting the word contemptuously off his tongue like he'd often done in days gone by. "*Outsider!* Get your machete and come out here! Come out and face me like a man! Let me test your strength!"

The women with Catalina looked at me nervously for some assurance that nothing would happen, but I had none. Considering the wild succession of improbabilities we had witnessed since Wishiquimi's injury, I did not feel qualified to hazard any guesses. I thought we had been prepared for the battle for souls, but I was overcome by the fury of the past few weeks. I wilted at the sight of Timoteo's anger and whispered to Wally that I had never seen him so enraged. He squeezed my hand. "You've got a poor memory," he said quietly.

"Timoteo!" Wally called through the window. "I didn't call you down here to have a fight! Come inside! I want to ask you something!"

"I'm not stepping into your house!" he yelled, "If you're afraid to come out and face me, I'm going back to the village."

"Go ahead," Wally answered. "If you're not coming in to talk, you may as well go."

Timoteo stalked angrily away for a moment, then turned to face the house again. "Why should I come in?" he called.

"So I can ask you about something."

"What about?" He walked back to the house, opened the door, and paused hesitantly on the threshold. He surveyed the silent crowd in the porch to determine whether or not they would interpret his return as weakness. They backed away as he entered. "What do you want?" he asked, avoiding Wally's gaze.

"These women were really angry at me," Wally said, nodding toward the frightened group huddled near the doorway. "Somebody told them I'd been accusing them of immorality behind their backs." Timoteo swung uneasily at the partition with his machete.

"I was angry."

"You must have been," Wally murmured. "Did you really say we doubt everyone's faith? Did you say we think you might as well return to the old way of life?"

Timoteo drew a deep breath and turned to face him. "Brother," he began slowly. "I just get upset when they gossip about Catalina all the time."

"Timoteo," Wally asked, "could it be that *you* want to go back to the old way?"

Timoteo seemed startled by the possibility. "No," he said. "Of course not." He studied Wally for a moment, wondering whether or not it would do any good to express his real confusion. "Wally," he finally said, "this is what I think. When I put my trust in Jesus Christ, my hunger for vengeance vanished. My anger disappeared. I thought to myself, *Well! My desires are new! God is really within me!* I was content, and I thought I'd always stay that way. But I don't. People anger me, and I feel like fighting. Then I think to myself, *Maybe I've just been deceiving myself.*" He stopped abruptly. "What do *you* think?" he asked Wally. "Could it be that I *am* deceiving myself?"

The violence of his arrival was gone, and it startled me that I could forget it so completely. Wally shook his head and put a hand on Timoteo's shoulder. "No," he assured him. "Don't feel that way. You belong to the Lord. If you weren't sincere, you wouldn't even be talking this way right now."

Timoteo nodded sober understanding as Wally explained how temptation was common to all mankind, and it seemed that the light began to dawn as they discussed the turmoil of events that had followed Wishiquimi's injury.

When Timoteo left a while later, he had a new understanding of the importance of living a consistent life. And I had a new respect for the power of the Gospel.

The situation slowly improved as different ones began to admit their responsibility in the problems they had experienced, and a

Tempted and Tried

few days later a group of them met with some Balafili families from Samuel's village to review their difficulties from beginning to end. Quite a crowd collected on a little knoll in front of our house, and though they subsequently congratulated themselves on the serenity of the meeting, an uninitiated observer would surely have trembled.

Two young men broke away from the gathering, wandered into our porch, and seated themselves on a bench by the fire. They were part of the group that had attacked Waldo's niece on the hillside during the days when Jaime's wife was still being withheld. They had often strolled around the house in an obvious attempt to strike up a conversation relevant to the offense they had committed; but so far they had never mustered sufficient courage to introduce the subject.

The first time they had returned to our house, Wally had asked them concerning the charges, and they had denied everything. We had decided then and there we would not bring up the subject again. We would treat them as innocent and wait for the Lord to work the necessary conviction in their hearts.

One of them finally came over to the partition and watched me work in the kitchen for a few moments before he asked where Wally was.

"Outside," I answered. "Shall I call him?"

He nodded miserably. "Ask me...uh...ask me..." he began, choking on every word while he tried to force himself to continue. "Ask me about that girl."

"Wally already asked you," I smiled. "You said it was a lie."

"Ask me again," he suggested. "I won't say that this time."

I put my work aside and dried my hands on a towel. "Has God forgiven you?" I asked him.

The back door slammed, and he looked up to see Wally coming in. "I don't know," he replied, holding his arms out to beckon Wally. "I keep praying, but I don't think my heart will ever come clean again. My happiness is gone."

His companion joined him at the partition and took over the conversation. "Wally," he whispered nervously. "I want to tell you

Treasures of Darkness

something. I don't feel very good."

"What's wrong?" Wally asked politely, though he had already guessed the topic under discussion.

He took a deep breath and plunged right in. "I keep wondering why I went with Waldo that day," he began, referring to the man who had planned the assault on his own niece. "Why did I ever join him? It wasn't that I wanted to." He stopped for a moment and tried to read Wally's reaction. "I didn't want to go with him. I was frightened. But he kept telling me God would never know.

"He caught the girl, and she screamed for help, but Waldo just laughed at her. I felt nauseated.

"As soon as we released her and started walking home again, Waldo changed his mind and said maybe God *would* find out. When I got to my shelter I couldn't eat. I knew God had seen us. I had known it all along. I lie in my hammock angrily, and my wife began to cry. She knew I'd done something wrong, and it frightened her. I tried to pray and ask the Lord to take away my guilt, but He wouldn't listen. I'm still unclean."

"Brother," he pleaded. "You tell Him for me. Ask Him to take away my sorrow. What's going to happen to me?"

My heart ached for him. His self-condemnation was more than he could bear, and I found myself increasingly indignant at the man I held responsible. I could have grabbed Waldo by the shoulders and shaken him. For weeks he had blatantly denied having done anything at all, and he laughed off the whole incident as the figment of someone's imagination. I turned back to the sink and clattered the pots and pans.

Wally encouraged them to trust the Lord for forgiveness and assured them that he would be praying for them. They finally left.

Waldo joined the men for a meeting a few days later and shuffled over to Wally to ask a question while the stragglers scrambled for seats. I could hear snippets of conversation as they whispered back and forth.

"Brother," Waldo began, grinning uneasily. "Is it true that a man who sins without feeling sorry doesn't really know the Lord?"

Wally said it was.

Tempted and Tried

"That frightens me," Waldo grimaced. "Don't talk that way."

"Why should it bother you?" Wally asked innocently.

Waldo did not answer right away. "Don't make me sad," he finally said. "I've already confessed my sin. I prayed last night." He paused to study Wally's response. "If you don't believe me, ask someone else," he said. "I didn't stay home and pray by myself. I went to Enrique's house when everyone was gathered there."

I studied his expression as he tried to persuade Wally of his sincerity and decided he was fortunate that God's forbearance was greater than mine.

After the meeting, a group of us were enjoying a late afternoon visit in front of the house when someone saw Samuel trooping in despondently from the airstrip. The past few weeks had been difficult for him, too, and he had not been immune to the tensions created by the friction between his village and the people of the big savannah. Someone had broken into a drum of trade goods we had left at our little shack in the Balafili valley, and Samuel had found an outlet for his emotions in a determined effort to apprehend the thief.

He lowered himself slowly to the pole beside us, tossed his bow and arrows to the ground, and moaned wearily as he rubbed the muscles of his legs. "Wally," he sighed, "my legs are so sore I can hardly stand. I've been traveling to every village day after day, trying to make someone confess to the theft, but everyone denies it."

He rested his elbows on his knees and cupped his chin in his hands. "I feel terrible," he groaned. "I've screamed myself hoarse. My throat hurts, my legs ache, and my back is sore. I'm so angry I can't even think straight. And my heart is upset and lonely."

"I know, I know," Enrique nodded. "That's how it happens. Anger makes you feel that way."

"Anger!" Samuel exclaimed. "Was I *ever* angry! I went to the closest village first, and they just *laughed* when I asked who'd broken into the drum. The old man there sat in his hammock and grinned at me, and I thought to myself, *I ought to go for the saw Wally left at my house and crack his head open.*

He caught the startled expression on my face and burst into laughter. "Margarita," he chuckled as his merriment subsided, "you wouldn't have recognized me! I looked at the old man's wife and thought to myself, *And if you so much as whimper for him, I'll whack off your fingers so you won't be able to wipe away your tears!*"

He dramatized his account with a lively demonstration of his annoyance, and he related his trials in a tense, high voice reserved for emotion-packed moments. Everyone smiled at the vivid portrayal he presented. Surrounded by such a sympathetic audience, he unwound with the telling of it.

By the time the tale was told, Samuel was laughing at himself. He rubbed his aching leg muscles. "But I can't argue like I used to," he sighed ruefully. "Every time I shout at someone I feel shaky inside."

There was silence for a few moments. That feeling was nothing new. "It happened to me once, too," Enrique nodded. "But when people prayed for me my strength returned."

Enrique stretched to his feet and grinned at the crowd with a confidence born of painful experience. "Come on," he suggested. "Let's make Samuel strong-hearted again. Let's go down to the village and call the people together."

9

A New Sun

The glory of the Lord is risen upon thee.

Isaiah 60:1

Manuela slipped into the porch with her new baby and waited anxiously on the fringe of the crowd that had just launched into their favorite song with blissful disregard for tune or tempo.

He wasn't afraid to die,
He did it for my cleansing.

"Margarita!" she whispered urgently as the tumult of their praise faded away. I motioned her to silence and pointed out a space on the crowded floor where she could sit with the others and wait until the close of the meeting. Her little girl was five days old, and I supposed she had brought her to the house for the customary bath and blanket I always gave to tiny new members of the community. But when she settled to the floor with the baby hugged to her breast, she began to cry.

In a moment all the women around her were in tears, and I stepped over the sprawl of legs and babies for a closer look. Manuela was trying to force milk into the baby's mouth in a pathetic attempt to sustain her life, but she did not seem to be accomplishing very much. No one seemed sure whether the child was dead or alive.

"Call the doctors! Where are the doctors?" the women began to wail. A medical team from the United States was with us for a few days doing research in the village, and one of them rushed to our

Treasures of Darkness

aid. He examined the baby and reached for a penicillin injection.

"Somebody better go for Bill," he said, referring to his colleague, a pediatrician who was collecting information in the roundhouse. "This baby's nearly gone."

Both lungs were completely congested, whether with pneumonia or milk he could not tell, and he offered very little hope of recovery. Manuela was terrified at the thought of offering up her tiny baby for an injection, but she was even more frightened by the doctor's diagnosis. She finally yielded her little one and wept in despair to see its lack of response to the needle. Not a whisper of resistance.

Dr. Bill soon came, and they studied his face carefully as he spread out his equipment and worked over the baby. He listened, he felt, he probed, but his expression was alarming. He shook his head. It seemed that the baby's heart was enlarged, and he doubted that normal breathing would have been possible regardless of the complications pneumonia might add. He handed the baby back to Manuela and suggested that we prepare them for the inevitable.

We turned to face the tear-stained mother, who was desperately hoping for good news. Wally's long silence frightened her. "The doctor says he can't do anything," he finally said. Manuela looked at him uncomprehendingly, then grasped the baby tightly to herself and sobbed uncontrollably.

She was from Miguel's village on the other side of the savannah, but the women crying around her coaxed her to spend the night with them. They promised to pray for the little one all night long. They left for the village, and Wally and I joined the doctors in the kitchen to listen to an explanation of what happens with enlargement of the heart.

I could not concentrate. I was too preoccupied with Manuela's sorrow, and my attention was toward the village. At any moment I expected to hear the piercing cry that would tell us that the end had come.

We could hear the sound of their prayers long after we had retired for the night. For a long time we lay awake wondering how to explain the fact that the Lord giveth and the Lord taketh away.

Early in the morning I awoke with a start. The sun was already

A New Sun

sending the first gray streaks of dawn across the savannah, and no one had called us all night. I jumped out of bed and went to the window. Everything was silent in the village. Dressing myself quickly, I hurried outside and clanged on the bell that called the sick to the dispensary.

Manuela was the first one there. Her face was streaked and her eyes were swollen, but the baby in her arms was breathing a little more easily. She smiled through her tears as her little one whimpered an objection to a second penicillin injection, then wrapping her securely in a blanket, she hurried back to the village.

The others who had not been so frantic for medical attention drifted in slowly for the next half hour. José was among them and once the women dispersed, he stepped forward for cough medicine.

"Hah!" he sighed, while Wally hunted for the cough syrup. "Would I love a good sleep! I hardly slept all night. Either I was sitting in Enrique's house praying for the baby, or I was swinging in my hammock listening to all the women cough." He gave a convincing demonstration, coughing and gagging till he threatened to come apart. "And now I've caught it."

"No wonder," Wally scolded, measuring the medicine into a spoon. "I told you colds would spread if you didn't quit sharing the same wads of tobacco."

"Ho! Is that why I'm sick?" José laughed, grinning into Wally's face and holding out his lower lip for inspection. "Do you see tobacco in there?"

"No, it's probably behind your ear," Wally suggested. "Or on your shoulder." Jose delightedly proved that it was not.

"I'm through," he whispered excitedly. "You won't find it anywhere. Not even in my garden!" He swallowed his medicine before he finished the story. "Brother, tobacco really made my mouth lazy. And it made my heart angry. I never felt like praying any more. All I wanted to do was lie in my hammock with a big wad of tobacco and ponder the evil anyone ever did against me." Wally nodded. Others had shared the same complaint. Tobacco seemed to be an emotional hazard.

Treasures of Darkness

"I prayed about it," José continued. "I said, Father, go ahead and destroy all my tobacco plants. I won't care. Make them wither.' But He didn't. So we went out and destroyed them ourselves.

"You should have seen us!" he grinned, delighting in the memory of his campaign. "We tore up the whole patch! We stomped it, pulled it up, slashed it, scattered it everywhere!" His smile faded, and he leaned forward. "But we also destroyed my father-in-law's crop," he added apologetically. "I was afraid it might tempt me."

"Wasn't he angry?" Wally asked, hardly able to keep from smiling at José's typical extremism.

José looked annoyed. Why should anyone begrudge a little hardship for so worthy a cause? "Just let him be angry," he answered, picking up his machete and heading for the door. "He'll get over it eventually."

We watched him disappear jauntily down the path, then we turned back to the dispensary table to clear the chaotic clutter of medicine bottles.

Two days passed, and convinced that her little one had begun a sure recovery, Manuela finally took her across the savannah to her own village. But the doctors did not share her optimism. The baby's initial response had been dramatic, but continued recovery seemed suspiciously slow. The pneumonia may have responded to antibiotics, but the problem did not end there.

A few days later the medical team was preparing to leave. The doctors were loading their luggage into the plane when Manuela hurried down the airstrip and approached us in tears. I was almost afraid to look at the baby she clutched to herself, but Dr. Bill opened his medical kit and prepared for one final examination.

"She's worse than ever," he sighed. "It's not the lungs; it's the heart. I can't be sure with so tiny a baby, but I really don't see any hope."

He handed the baby back to Manuela, repacked his equipment, and headed for the plane. I followed after him, desperate for a word of hopeful advice, and Manuela called out after us in panic, "Don't walk away! Don't turn your back on me! Don't say my little

A New Sun

one is hopeless!" I hurried back to her and asked her to sit quietly until the plane left.

We finally returned to the porch to face Manuela and the crowd of sympathizers that had gathered around her. They shifted a little to make room for Wally and silently awaited the doctor's verdict. "The heart is too big," Wally began, groping for words that would make the news less painful. "The baby's lungs are too crowded. They haven't got space to function properly."

The sober crowd around him nodded their understanding and waited for him to tell them how he proposed to correct the situation. "I could give more penicillin," Wally suggested lamely. "Just for something to do."

"What do you mean? What are we supposed to do?" they whispered in frightened confusion. "What did the doctor say?"

"He said the little one will soon be gone."

It was out. For a moment they seemed stunned. Then they nodded their heads grimly. No wonder the doctors had been so anxious to leave. They were trying to avoid a hopeless situation the way a frustrated witchdoctor might have done.

"Well, can't *you* do something?" they asked incredulously. "You're not going to help us?"

They could not fathom such fatalistic acceptance of the doctor's verdict. Were we not the ones who had taught them of God's power? I struggled with conflicting emotions. I was angry at their stubborn refusal to accept the inevitable and uneasy at their disappointment with our lack of faith.

"We don't know *how* to make anyone's heart smaller," I insisted defensively. I was on the verge of tears. "Even the *doctors* don't know how to do that." The women began to cry, and the men studied us with increasing annoyance.

"Well then we'll look after her ourselves," said one, in exasperation. He stood to his feet and turned toward the door. "Let him give her another injection," he said to Manuela. "And then bring her down to the village."

Once more we spent a sleepless night, tossing restlessly to and fro while we awaited the piercing wail from the village. We prayed that the Lord would grant them the serenity to accept it graciously. And once more the night passed with no panicky pounding on the door.

Lord, I prayed, as I scrambled into my clothes the following morning, *can she still be alive?* I struggled for assurance but could not quite grasp the confidence I wanted. Surely He would not tease us by merely prolonging the agony. I was overwhelmed with awesome respect for the faith of the people in the roundhouse.

Enrique followed Manuela to the dispensary and told us how they had spent the night praying in shifts. One by one they had taken their place by Manuela's hammock, rubbed the sleep from their eyes, and petitioned the Lord to squeeze the baby's heart to a smaller size. When sleep would threaten to overtake them, they would call for a fresh volunteer to continue the chain of prayer. No one considered it a burdensome task. They enjoyed a challenge anyway, and their faith was not hampered by a confusing reliance on medical science.

Manuela brought her baby back in the evening, and we scrounged through our medical supplies until we found a few bottles of pediatric drops for respiratory problems. They did not seem to feel so discouraged anymore. I felt ashamed for having despaired when hope was most needed, but they did not seem to resent it at all. They accepted our weaknesses as we did theirs and shared the joy of victory with us as though we were equal partners in faith. It was a very humbling experience.

Wally was working at his desk with an informant a few days later when Manuela poked her head through the doorway and asked if she could step inside for a moment. She smiled down at the baby snuggled contentedly in her arms. "Look at her!" she whispered. "She's breathing normally!"

"She's fine," Wally agreed. "You might as well take her back to your own village again." Manuela smiled widely. That was what she had been hoping he would say.

"Keep praying for her anyway," she whispered shyly, as she let herself out the door.

Wally pushed his chair back from the desk and ordered a cup of

A New Sun

coffee. Waldo, who had been helping him check out some recent translation, grinned in anticipation. Coffee break was his favorite interlude. "What shall we talk about?" he asked. They always used such intermissions to discuss tribal concepts of the world.

"Let me ask you about the sun," Wally suggested. "Where does it go in the evening?" He knew they had no concept of a spherical earth to explain the sun's reappearance every morning. "What happens to it?"

Waldo laughed self-consciously, wondering about the acceptability of his theory. "We say it goes into a hole," he smiled.

"How does it get out again?" Wally asked. "Does it sneak back to the other side in the darkness?"

"No," Waldo laughed. "It stays there. It's gone. The sun the next morning is a new one. There's a different sun every day."

I do not know exactly what it was, but something about his concept appealed to me as wonderfully refreshing. Perhaps it was because I was reminded of the new sun that was dawning on the big savannah—the new light that was piercing the darkness.

I carried the coffee to the front room and smiled at the remembrance of the new sun the prophet Malachi had predicted. How fitting Malachi 4:2 seemed! *"Unto you that fear my name shall the Sun of righteousness arise with healing in His wings!"*

Everyone squeezed closer to study the pictures Wally held as he taught the details surrounding Saul's conversion. "So he went to the river with Ananias," he said. "And there he was baptized." He turned the page to an illustration of two men standing in the water, and paused a moment as a flurry of excited whispers broke forth. All were anxious to explain baptism to the visitors Pedro had brought to the village, and the new arrivals struggled to understand the symbolism depicted on the paper before them.

Pedro had just returned from a long trip where he had shared the Gospel with villages beyond the western ridge and with others in the north. Two young couples, eager to learn more of the words that promised eternal life, had accompanied him back to the big savannah. Now plans were being made for a large expedition to join them for their return trip. Many had reportedly turned to the

Lord in their village, and David and Enrique wanted to spend six weeks or so among them to encourage them in their new faith.

"Wally," Enrique said, "were *you* ever baptized?"

"Sure," Wally answered. "Both of us were. When we were teenagers."

"Ha! That's the way!" Enrique grinned. "That's what *we're* going to do, too! Old people, young people, everybody who loves the Lord! As soon as we get back from our trip we'll invite all our friends for a baptismal service!"

"OK," Wally nodded, smiling at the enthusiasm Enrique's suggestion was creating. We had been teaching on baptism for a long time already, and many were eagerly awaiting the day they could step into the stream in public declaration of faith in Christ.

It had been Paul and Marty who initiated the interest in baptism, and for their sakes we had been trying to postpone the service until they returned with Wishiquimi. But we did not feel we could wait much longer. Some had already decided the baptism had been delayed too long and had baptized one another in the swamp one afternoon.

The meeting dispersed, and a sprinkling of Balafili visitors stayed to talk after the others had left. Samuel wanted to know when we were planning another trip to their area, and Wally told them we would try to get over for a visit as soon as the Shadles returned with the girl we had sent out to the hospital. The mention of Wishiquimi caused an uneasy silence for a moment or two.

"How is she?" Samuel asked. "Did they cut it off?"

Wally shook his head. "No," he assured them. "Paul called us on the radio and said the doctors are going to operate instead. They've just sent her to a larger hospital, where someone is going to fasten the broken bone with a piece of metal. They say she'll be able to walk again." Samuel nodded with relief. If she returned with the use of both legs, there probably would not be any more hard feelings.

A few days later, a large group of men, women, and children accompanied the northern visitors back over the mountains on their long, homeward journey. Those who could read were armed

A New Sun

with copies of all the Bible story booklets we had in print, and those who could not were equipped with illustrated editions that did not require a literate teacher.

Miguel's people caught their enthusiasm and set off to the regions beyond on an evangelistic trip of their own. As soon as they returned, they hurried across the savannah to report on their experiences. For some, it had been their first attempt at sharing the Gospel, and their excitement was boundless. Their eagerness had compensated for their lack of theological expertise. We joined them on the porch to hear the details of their adventure.

Miguel listed the villages they had reached, counting them off on his fingers and sharing the news that even the most remote groups had wanted to know all about the message they had come to share. "We talked until we were hoarse," he laughed. "And still, every time we'd say 'That's all for now,' the old men would interrupt and say, 'Little Ones, tell us more.' We told them to turn from witchcraft and be washed in the blood of God's Son, so they would not be left behind when Jesus returned."

He paused for a moment to catch his breath, and Manuela's husband broke into the monologue to add his own impressions. "They're friendly!" he exclaimed. "Really and truly friendly! We used to be *enemies*!" Miguel laid a hand on his shoulder to silence him so he could continue his own account.

"We got to a distant village where I hadn't been since I was young," he continued. "And we were sitting in the clearing with a group of men when visitors from Bolewateli arrived!"

"Ho! What happened?" Wally whispered. We had never met the Bolewateli people, but their ferocity was legendary, and Miguel's people had had a long history of warfare with them before our arrival.

Miguel breathlessly dramatized the encounter. His voice fell to a whisper and rose to a high-pitched falsetto as he described the tension of the first moments. "We shouted and screamed at one another," he said. "And we brought up all our old grudges and accusations. Then I calmed myself. 'Listen to us, Father,' I said to one old man. 'Don't accuse *us* of anyone's death. Your sadness isn't

Treasures of Darkness

our fault. We don't even *do* witchcraft anymore. We're peaceful toward everyone.'"

"We told them how we serve the Lord now," Miguel's brother interrupted. "We told them Jesus died and came back to life. We taught them about eternal life and God's protection. They kept saying 'Ho! That sounds like it could be the truth.'"

Everyone wanted to talk at once. Manuela's husband broke into the conversation again, still exclaiming over the reception they had received. "I *never* thought I'd enter the village of my enemies! I *never* thought I'd speak with them face to face! And they invited us back in ten days to teach them more!"

"We're going, too!" Miguel's brother announced, stomping his feet and slapping himself on the thigh. "We're going in ten days, and they want us to bring all the books we can get!" He burst into an enthusiastic dance and hooted his joy to the world. "So give us a job!" he laughed. "What can we do to earn some books? Carry water? Clear ground? We'll need all the books you have!"

They finally exhausted the news of their travels and reminded Wally that he had promised to teach them something new when they returned. But they had barely begun when someone ran from the roundhouse with the news that scores of visitors were approaching from the north. David and Enrique were returning with a large group of followers from the northern villages.

The congregation scrambled to their feet and rushed to the village to join the welcoming committee. We followed along to join in the festivities, but while we were still crossing the swamp, the screams and shouts of the welcome chorus rose in a deafening roar.

The following afternoon, Enrique brought the visitors to the porch for a meeting. He introduced them according to village affiliation, and pointed out those who were already Christians. The line of demarcation seemed to be well defined in his mind, but it sounded too good to be true. I was thankful Enrique could not see the skepticism I felt as I studied their faces and wondered whether the light of the gospel had really penetrated their hearts.

The meeting began, and Enrique suggested that the visitors pray

A New Sun

first. What a thrill I felt, in the stillness of that meeting, to hear the Gospel unfold from the lips of men who had never known contact with the outside world! One by one they prayed to their heavenly Father with a freedom that left little doubt of their sincerity, and throughout their prayers were woven the stories of creation, of Noah, of Elijah, of Jonah, of Lazarus, of the parables, of Christ's death and resurrection, and of His second coming.

"Wow!" Wally whispered, when the last amen had sounded. "They must have spent the whole six weeks teaching!"

David stretched to his feet and hitched up the droopy pants that had become his mark of distinction. Those who always wore clothing were still a decided minority. "Brother," he grinned, "here we are! When shall we be baptized?!"

"Whenever you want to," Wally laughed. They decided to plan the meeting for two days later. That would give them time to take care of the necessary harvesting and gardening that had been neglected during their absence. Some were delegated to inform Miguel's people of the proposed service, some volunteered to invite the closest Shamatali village, and someone suggested including their friends of the Balafili valley.

When plans were complete, the crowd dispersed, and Enrique left with a stack of booklets designed to teach the mechanics and symbolism of baptism. With only two days to go, he did not have long to prepare his new converts!

The morning sky was bright and clear, and the people hurried to finish the day's work while the sun was still high. José rushed past the house with smoldering firebrands to kindle a fire in a new garden plot still cluttered with dead, dry wood. Timoteo and his wife hurried to their garden for a stalk of plantains. Firewood was chopped, fresh water was carried, and whatever clothing was available was laid out in readiness for the afternoon.

All available scraps of cloth were snatched up and sewn into skirts and hats, and strips of bright material too narrow for anything else were tied decoratively around arms, heads, and ankles. Even the stream that had served adequately for years of bathing, drinking, hunting crabs, and skinning frogs was given a face-lift in honor of the occasion. Juan and Rosito splashed enthusiastically into the cold waters and began a boisterous campaign to rid the riverbed of all debris that might cause the old women to stumble.

A delegation from the village arrived to say they would be ready to begin the service early in the afternoon. I relayed their message to Wally, who was poring over a partially translated hymn in the next room, and returned with his reply. "That's too early," I said. "We've been announcing the meeting for the late afternoon, and now Wally has started something he can't quit. And anyway," I added, "you agreed to call the meeting at the regular time when we all discussed it a couple of days ago."

"Yes, but now we don't want to wait that long. We won't have time if we put it off until the sun is low," Enrique explained. "And the water gets cold later on."

"Be that as it may," I shrugged. "Wally's busy with translation and says he can't stop in the middle of it."

He studied my face for a moment, trying to determine his chances of changing my mind, and then nodded with annoyed resignation. "Ho," he answered and led his silent companions out the door.

I assured Wally that all was going according to schedule, but early in the afternoon a colorful band of more than two hundred passed by the house, and Enrique returned with a determined group of village dignitaries. "Where's Wally?" he asked.

"In there," I said, nodding toward the next room. "He's still writing."

"Tell him I want him."

I passed on the message, floundering a little when Wally reminded me that I had said everything was under control. "They're going to have to learn a little self-discipline," he insisted. "They've got to respect the schedules they agree to. I'm not just sitting around waiting for something to happen. I'm *busy*!"

"OK," I said. "But everyone has already gone to the stream."

I passed the message over the partition to the crowd in the

porch. They looked at one another impatiently.

"Wally!" David shouted. "Wally! Come here!"

"Wally!" Enrique echoed. "Are you coming with us? We're on our way to the stream to start the baptismal service."

There was a long pause from the next room, and I went to the doorway to see what possible answer might be forthcoming. Wally grinned at me for a moment before he shoved back his chair and got to his feet. "They can't do this to me!" he protested, with mock frustration. "Don't they know I'm a *missionary*?" I murmured my sympathy.

"That's the thanks I get," he continued, happily collecting the papers scattered over his desk. "I try to get them to take some responsibility, and what do they do? They take it!"

"I'll be right there!" he hollered to Enrique.

The people had collected near the bank of the stream and seated themselves on either side of the path, men on one side and women on the other. Enrique stood in the midst of them, directing traffic. "Wally! Right over here!" he said as we approached. The women grabbed at me as I passed by, and I allowed myself to be dragged to the ground beside Laughing Lady. Everyone shifted closer to make me feel welcome.

Late arrivals continued to drift in, and a group representative of ten separate villages had finally assembled on the grassy bank. The hubbub faded to a relative silence as the meeting got under way. After a few men led in prayer, Wally stepped down into the water and called for Enrique to follow him.

Enrique walked to Wally's side and folded his arms tightly across his chest the way the Philippian jailer had done in the pictures we had used. Holding him securely with one hand over his folded arms and the other behind him, Wally addressed him in a voice loud enough for all to hear. "Because you love my Father, God," he began, "and because the blood of His Son has taken away your sin, and because His Spirit indwells you, I'm putting you under the water so all will know you want to be obedient to Him." And with that he was baptized.

"Who's next?" Wally said. With a wide smile, Rosito jumped into the water, and the men began lining up along the shore. Enrique headed for the bank, then halted as Wally asked him to stay. He watched while Rosito was baptized, and when David stepped into the stream, Enrique moved quickly to his side.

David folded his arms across his chest, hesitated, and glanced toward Wally for a word of encouragement. "Like this?"

"Show him how." Wally nodded to Enrique. "And hold him just as I held you." Then Wally placed his hands over Enrique's, and David was baptized between the two of them.

Before long, Wally had worked himself out of a job. He sat on the bank with the others, keeping a watchful eye on the proceedings. One by one, the candidates for baptism stepped forward and took their place between David and Enrique. To each one, they offered a few timely exhortations before pronouncing the final words and dipping them under the water.

"Surely not *you*!" Enrique spluttered, as a young girl we had nicknamed Toughie stepped into the stream. "Since when do you care about following the Lord!?"

"She does! She does!" the "baptismal committee" shouted from the shore. "She asked the Lord to put her on the narrow way while you were visiting the northern villages, and she's been meeting with us ever since. Go ahead! Baptize her!"

Enrique studied the crowd lined up along the bank of the stream, and decided he had better accept their advice. Heads were nodding vigorously, and everyone began to smile as Enrique turned back to Toughie and motioned for her to come forward. She stood shyly between David and Enrique and nodded meekly at their suggestions that she behave herself from henceforth and stop flirting with the boys.

Because modesty discouraged physical contact between the sexes, and tribal taboos forbade any communications between certain in-laws, a flurry of excitement arose as the women began to step forward for baptism. Miguel hurried into the water to assist David and Enrique, and between the three of them they were able to keep confusion to a minimum by each baptizing the ones to whom they were most closely related. Three categories seemed

A New Sun

sufficient to include everyone, and things went smoothly until a visiting woman from the northern villages jumped eagerly into the stream.

She quickly waded toward the man closest to her, and Enrique's eyes widened in panic as she approached him. He held his ground rigidly, and the others watched in silent fascination. Her eyes were set on the swirling water around her, and she completely forgot the caution that would normally have prevented such a cultural blunder. Not until she found herself looking up into Enrique's startled face did she realize that she had approached the wrong man.

Enrique was every inch a gentleman. He promptly turned his back on her and folded his arms tightly across his chest to make sure he did not accidentally bump against her. She took her cue from him and turned around also.

Back to back they stood in the stream while Enrique spoke a few words of encouragement, urging her to keep her heart steadfast on the Lord. Then he turned quickly, grabbed her by the shoulders, and shoved her under the water in what must surely have been the fastest baptism on record!

Young and old, strong and lame, family groups, and solitary figures stepped forward for baptism. Miguel smiled as he watched his children lead his mother to the stream. She was a matriarch of the village, with wrinkled, leathery skin and squinting eyes. Her sight and hearing were nearly gone, and a recent illness had left her weak and wobbly.

Miguel and Enrique helped her into position, loudly explained the meaning of baptism, and suggested she keep her mouth shut. "Because you love my Father, God," Miguel began, and I smiled at her serenity as she shivered in the water and repeated the words her son spoke.

"Yes, I love Him," she nodded. "His blood has made me clean. His Spirit is within me."

"Old woman!" Enrique shouted into her ear, holding her steady against the current. "Keep your mouth shut now! You're going under!" And soon she was shaking the water vigorously from her

Treasures of Darkness

hair and reaching out for the helping hands that pulled her up the slippery slope.

The sun was almost gone. A chilly breeze sprang up, and everyone nodded quick agreement that others wishing to be baptized should wait for another day. The crowd began to disappear, and as Wally and I headed slowly for the house, we could hear the men planning an evening celebration. A meeting in Enrique's house would bring the day to a fitting conclusion.

10

Sweet Sorrow

Now unto Him that is able to keep you from falling . . . be glory and majesty, dominion and power.

Jude 24-25

I hurried down the path to the village, picked my way over the slim pole that bridged the swamp, and clumsily jumped across the mud holes on the trail that led to higher ground. I reached the brow of the knoll, and paused for a moment's reflection as the village came into view.

Thin columns of smoke sifted through blackened roofs, and the sound of children playing in the village clearing drifted across the savannah. A dog yelped; a man's voice hooted in laughter. My eyes wandered from shelter to shelter, reliving the memories each home held, and they came to rest on the dilapidated barricade that had once been so carefully maintained to protect them against their enemies. It did not matter that the village palisade had crumbled in ruins. No more raiders came to the big savannah.

A little girl appeared behind José's shelter and startled me out of my reverie with an excited squeal. She dashed back into the village to announce my arrival, and I turned my attention back to the business at hand. Our scheduled furlough was only weeks away, and there was no time for sentimental journeys back through the past three years.

A group of children ran out to meet me as I approached Octavio's shelter, and they offered me a piece of firewood as

Treasures of Darkness

defense against the dogs.

"Did you bring medicine for my mother?" a little boy whispered, bouncing up and down beside me while he kept a firm hold on my arm. I raised my eyebrows in an affirmative gesture, and he hurried to his mother's hearth to pass on the good news.

She smiled as she pulled herself into an upright position and carefully unwrapped the bandage that bound her leg. I settled down on a piece of firewood beside her hammock and reached for the can of medicine I carried. "And how is our little one's mother today?" I asked, as the women from nearby shelters crowded around. The patient answered for herself.

"A little better," she groaned, sighing her pleasure as I poured a little hydrogen peroxide into the gash below her knee.

Some women from the visiting northern villages approached us skeptically to offer candid appraisals of my ability. They cautioned the group against entrusting medical responsibilities to ignorant 'outsiders,' but they were promptly silenced by the loud insistence of the others that our treatments were highly effective. Nor could they comprehend the concern of those who studied me with misty eyes and asked how many days it would be before the plane came to take us away.

I packed the medicine and began to stretch to my feet. "Don't go yet," one of the older women whispered, gently pulling me into a ragged bark hammock beside her. She wrapped her arms around me. "Why do you want to make us cry?" she asked. "Do you think we won't be lonely? Do you think your departure won't affect the men? They're going to be upset when Wally leaves." The others crowded closer, nodding tearful agreement. All but the visitors.

"She's just an outsider, isn't she?" one of them asked with puzzled annoyance. "They're not Yanoamö are they, that you should cry for them?"

"Oh, you wouldn't understand," the woman with the sore leg answered impatiently. "We call her 'sister'." That was supposed to explain everything, but judging by the perplexity on the faces of the visitors, it was far from satisfactory.

I watched the women of the big savannah struggle to explain the

Sweet Sorrow

bonds that had grown between us and realized I would soon be facing a similar situation myself. I could already hear our Canadian friends and relatives asking incredulously, "Can you really get *close* to people like them?"

I blinked back the tears and put the subject of our departure out of my mind.

With only a few more days to go until the plane arrived, activity came to a standstill, and the people congregated around the house all day, asking questions.

"Brother," Waldo began, "does Cecilio talk all right?" He was referring to Cecil Neese, who was to move into our house during our year of furlough.

"You already know him," Wally said. "You've talked with him before."

"But we don't understand him very well. He talks like you used to."

"Then teach him to talk better."

"Sure," Enrique nodded. "We've already taught Wally. We won't have any trouble teaching Cecilio."

They did not all accept the idea with such enthusiasm. "I'm tired of teaching people," one of them grumbled. "We just get Wally speaking properly and another one comes."

"Wally," David's brother said, leaning over the partition to command his full attention, "put that down for a minute and listen to me. Will Cecilio know the answers? If we ask him what God says, will he be able to tell us?"

They had questions concerning Cecil's ability to treat sickness and his wife's proficiency at sewing. They wondered if Cecil knew how to hunt with a shotgun and whether their babies would be afraid of new outsiders. "And what about our matches—and thread—and axes? Where will we be able to get things when you're gone?"

Wally assured them that the Neeses would bring trade items, and then a flurry of excitement started as they wondered how they would pay for the things they wanted. All they had was the money *we'd* given them through trade.

Treasures of Darkness

"That's all right," Wally said. "He'll accept that."

"Really? Won't he say 'this ugly stuff isn't mine'? Won't it make you angry if we pass on your money to somebody else?"

They settled down again to discuss the problems that had been bothering them at the thought of having to "switch" outsiders, and Wally turned away shaking his head. "Given a little time," he laughed, "they'd devise a system of inviting a guest missionary to speak, and then they'd vote on him and offer him a 'call'!"

The final morning came, and the radio informed us that the plane was already on its way. The porch was crowded from sunup with various groups that took turns sitting in doleful huddles and recalling what they considered to be the highlights of our stay. They remembered the fear they had felt when they first saw the plane and heard its roar. They smiled at the memory of the amusement we had afforded them during the first days, their annoyance with us when we had insisted on charging for the things we gave them, and their anger at our reluctance to help them wipe out their enemies from the Balafili valley.

"Wally," Enrique said, "how long will it be before Paul and Marty come back?"

"They'll be here by the time the next moon is full," he guessed. "Wishiquimi can't walk yet. She's doing fine, but they have to wait a little longer."

"How many days before Cecilio and his wife come?"

"About ten."

Enrique shifted his weight from one foot to the other. He was running out of conversation pieces. "Wally," he said, after a lengthy pause, "we're going to miss you."

"We'll be lonesome, too."

The silence was difficult. The men were too upset to speak. They sat in a silent row, looking at Wally.

Finally Enrique decided something had to be done about the overwhelming sadness that was developing. "Brother," he laughed, "I know what you're going to do when you get back to your own country–you're going to hug your mother-in-law!"

Everyone howled with laughter, and they all hid their faces in

Sweet Sorrow

embarrassment at the very thought of it. They never had reconciled themselves to the fact that outsiders were not afraid of their in-laws, and they laughingly recalled the day Marty Shadle's mother had visited the big savannah and greeted Paul with an embrace!

The distant roar of a plane interrupted the conversation, and we assembled in front of the house to await its arrival.

No one smiled the usual greeting to pilot Jim Hurd as he stepped from the plane. His appearance was usually cheered enthusiastically, but this time he was the villain.

The women gathered protectively around me, staring at me silently and warning each other not to make me cry. "Sister," one of them whispered, reaching out to take my hand. Two big tears rolled down her cheeks and melted my composure. I could not hold back the tears.

"Look what you've done!" one of the men shouted. "We told you not to make her cry! Get out of here!" The women scattered, and I withdrew into the house. I leaned against the partition and gazed through the window at the green hills of the big savannah. How I would miss them!

The door opened gently, and Enrique's mother shuffled into the porch. She suddenly seemed old and feeble. Her head was bowed, and she did not speak until she was standing beside me. I felt miserable. I was ready to call the whole thing off and unpack my suitcase. I had a hunch that whatever she said was going to unlock the floodgates.

"Child," she whispered, "is it true?"

My tongue would not operate. She put her hands on my arms, and I nodded my head numbly. She began to cry softly, and at the sound of her weeping, the door opened a crack and one of the women peeked in.

"It's Enrique's mother and Margarita!" she called to the rest. "They're crying together!" That was all it took. From then on, any semblance of order was purely coincidental. Enrique rushed into the porch to rescue me, but a second later he was backing out the door shaking his head.

Time came for boarding the plane, and I moved outside with the

Treasures of Darkness

children, only to be surrounded by another mournful group. I told myself their tears were just a formality, but I could not really believe it.

"Margarita," someone said, and I turned to face Manuela and her miracle baby. It had been three months now since the Lord had squeezed the little one's heart to a smaller size. Manuela had come across the savannah to see if it was true that we were really leaving. "I just came to see..." she began, then burst into tears. The answer was obvious. She spun on her heel and fled to the Shadles' house, where she huddled against a wall and watched from a distance.

We climbed aboard the plane, and the men moved forward to surround us in a silent, sober circle. They did not cry. They *would* not cry. They assumed stoic, angry postures—manly postures—and spoke not a word to one another nor to us. Wally tried to say goodbye to them, but none could find words to answer him. Behind them the women hugged their babies to themselves for consolation, and cried brokenheartedly. I wept at the sight of them, and Davey snuggled up against me, wondering what was happening to his mother.

Jim Hurd looked around the circle of men and asked Wally who was going to pray. Enrique volunteered. "Father, God," he began, "take care of them while they're away, and bring them back before we despair."

I could not concentrate on his prayer. There was too much about the setting that took me back three years to the day of our arrival. The same plane on the same sunny savannah, the mountains round about, the people milling round. *Yanoamö Paradise*—the phrase flashed across my mind, and I recalled the laughter it had caused in those first days when the big savannah had seemed anything but heavenly. It did not seem so funny anymore.

I stole a glance at the crowd around the plane. Years had diminished the original cast. Julio did not stand beside José. Scar Shoulder was gone. Ramón was missing.

Timoteo leaned against the side of the plane with his head bowed. José stood beside him, his hands wrapped tightly around the bow and arrows clasped to his chest. My eyes wandered to the

Sweet Sorrow

stump of a finger, a silent reminder of the days when he first began to sense his need of the Lord.

They were surrounded by the crowd of ex-witchdoctors and warriors who had met us with weapons and war paint. I agonized over their future for a moment, wondering what unforeseen trials lay in store for them. They were so explosive, so extreme!

"Father," Enrique continued, "we're Yours. If You hadn't sent us the words of eternal life, we'd still be sitting on the brink of hell. We'd still be killing each other. No one but You could have given us peace. Take care of us while we're alone. Keep us from the sounds that lead in paths of violence. You're the One who's able."

The words of his prayer were strangely soothing, and I was filled with an overwhelming gratitude. I had seen Him touch the big savannah, and I treasured every memory. *Yes, You're the One who's able,* I echoed. *You're the One who's building Your Church, and not even the gates of hell can prevail against it. For the kingdom is Yours*

and the power
and the glory
forever and ever.
Amen.

Made in United States
Orlando, FL
06 February 2022